A Taste of Thailand

The Complete Thai Cookbook with More Than 300 Authentic Thai
Recipes!

Urassaya Manaying

TABLE OF CONTENTS

INTRODUCTION

If you've ever been to an authentic Thai restaurant, you already know that Thai food is all about a delicious balance between the five flavors- sweet, sour, salty, spicy, and bitter. Most recipes contain at least one ingredient for each of these flavors. Once you get used to Thai cooking, you will get a hang of Thai ingredients. You will get a sense of what ingredient does what, and how much of it you like in a particular recipe. You will then see the recipes in this book as a blank canvas, and tweak them to your, or your family's preferences. Let your instincts guide you, once you get a hang of things.

Each dish has a balance of ingredients, but a Thai meal too needs to be balanced as a whole, with a good variety of dishes that complement each other. For instance, if you're cooking a spicy curry, you will do well to serve a plain vegetable stir-fry on the side. It is also common for the Thai dinner table to have a few common taste making condiments so the individuals having the dinner can tweak the flavor of any dish to their liking. For example, vinegar, tamarind water and lime juice are common sour ingredients on the Thai dinner table.

Thai people enjoy food with a wide spectrum of ingredients, including seafood, meat, fruit, and vegetables. Here in Thailand, we like to enjoy what is in season, and what is available at hand in the kitchen. If we're short on an ingredient, we usually improvise.

You might find a few ingredients in this book that are hard to find. When in doubt, google the ingredient, and find a substitution. Some of the greatest recipes in the world are known to us today because someone, somewhere, improvised! So, feel free to improvise yourself. I know you'll need to.

Also, the amount of ingredients used are to my personal taste. Feel free to tweak any taste making ingredient to your own personal taste if you find the flavor too strong or too bland. It is always a good idea to start with less, as more spice can be added later, but it is impossible to remove it once it is in. You'll know the quantities you need to throw in for best results, after you've cooked a recipe once or twice.

Each recipe has "Yield" mentioned at the end. These are approximate, and since we Thai people like to enjoy multiple dishes in one meal, one serving of one dish might not be enough to satiate your hunger. Most recipes in this book are meant to be accompanied by rice.

The most important thing is to enjoy the process of Thai cooking. Follow your instincts, and let your creativity run wild!

WEATHER

Thailand enjoys a monsoon climate. The peninsula has two seasons: wet from November-July, and dry from August-October. The mainland has three seasons: wet from May-November, dry and cool from November-February, and dry and hot from March-April. If you're from a cold country, however, you might say that the weather here is hot and humid all year round.

AGRICULTURE

Thailand's fertile delta region is complemented by its hot and humid climate, yielding perfect agricultural conditions. Some archeologists even believe that central Thailand was the site of the first true agriculture on the planet and that rice has been cultivated there since between 4000 and 3500 B. C. Agricultural products make up 66 percent of the country's exports, and produces more than a third of the world's rice. Other prominent products are coconut, tapioca, rubber, sugar, pineapple, jute, soybeans, and palm oil. Two-thirds of the Thai labor force is engaged in agriculture.

FOOD CULTURE

As we talked before, Thai food is all about balancing sweet, salty, sour, bitter, and hot flavors. Not only the dishes, but the whole meal needs to be balanced with a delicious combinations of all these flavors. A few of the most popular taste makers and flavoring agents in Thai cooking are: coconut, lime, chili, garlic, ginger, cilantro, and dried fish (to make fish sauce). These ingredients are the foundation of Thai flavors.

As with food of any other region, Thai food has a few foreign influences. Chilies were introduced to Asia by the Portuguese in the 16th century, and this hot ingredient became a favorite of the Thai people, and a staple in the Thai kitchen. Hence, the Portuguese have had a huge influence on Thai cuisine. China and their stir-frying cooking techniques too have had a great influence on Thai cuisine. Indian curries and Indonesian spices are quite popular here too.

Thailand enjoys a huge coastline, making seafood a staple. Freshwater fish are super popular here too. Fish sauce is an indispensable part of Thai cuisine, and is used as a sauce, condiment, salt substitute, general taste maker, and flavoring agent. Dried fish are a popular snack in the country.

The country has a tropical climate, which leads to a limitless supply of delicious and exotic fruits and vegetables that are used in pretty much every kind of dish, and sometimes eaten by themselves too. The most important agricultural produce of Thailand is rice. Rice is also the most important and most common ingredient in Thai cuisine. In Thailand, the white and fragrant rice varieties are considered the best. Jasmine rice is a long-grained rice that is one of the favorite varieties here.

Most of the people in Thailand are Theravada Buddhists, and for them killing of animals is forbidden, but eating them is allowed. Regardless, meat is not a very common ingredient in the Thai cuisine, and is considered by most a special and rare treat. The meat that is served is often shredded.

In Thailand, all courses are usually served at once, so that the cook can enjoy the meal with his/her guests. Condiments such as dried chilies, chili paste, chopped peanuts, soy sauce, fish sauce, etc. are present on the table so the diners can tweak the flavor of a dish if they wish to.

Loaded with fish, vegetables, fruits, and rice, and low in meats and dairy, Thai cuisine is one of the healthiest in the world. Thai food is rich in carotinoids, flavonoids, and antioxidative vitamins, all known to have anti-cancer properties. It is no surprise that the Thai have the lowest rates of digestive tract cancer in the world.

THAI COOKING BASICS

Before we dive into the recipes, let us take a look at a few guidelines that might make your cooking experience a little better. These are quite basic, and if you've had some experience of following cookbooks in the past, you can skip them.

1. Read the recipe completely at least once before you start.
2. Make sure you have all the ingredients and tools needed for the recipe ready before you begin.
3. Fresh seasonal ingredients are always best.
4. Do all the cutting, chopping, and weighing the ingredients before you begin cooking.
5. Homemade ingredients are almost always better than store bought ones.
6. When measuring dry ingredients, level them off using the straight edge of a knife.
7. Use standard measuring spoons, cups, etc.

8. Rinse all vegetables and fruits meticulously and pat or spin dry.
9. Take meat out of the fridge approximately 15 minutes before cooking it, letting it come to room temperature. It will cook faster and more uniformly.
10. Use freshly ground pepper, if possible. Pepper starts to lose its flavor and pungency the moment it is ground.

BASIC COOKING METHODS

Here we will discuss a few of the most common cooking methods used in Thai cooking. Thai cooking is usually quite simple, and the methods used here are not much different from those used in the rest of the world.

STIR-FRYING AND SAUTÉING

These are identical cooking techniques that involve cooking in an open pan over high temperatures and with a negligible amount of cooking oil. Sautéing is usually done in either a slope-sided gourmet pan (or frying pan) or a straight-sided sauté pan. Stir-frying done in a wok.

These techniques are great for browning all kinds of meats.

Cooking fats must be relatively tasteless and have a high point. My favorites are canola oil and peanut oil. The oil must but not be smoking before you start to cook. To check, you can drizzle drop or two of water into the pan: It should spatter. Please be cautious as spatters can burn! Shaking the pan for sautéing or swiftly tossing ingredients in stir-frying prevents the food from adhering while it sears.

GRILLING AND BROILING

Grilling and broiling are cooking techniques in which food is cooked by exposing it to direct (often intense) heat over hot coals or some other heat source. This method is usually fast; the direct heat chars surface of the food, imparting delicious flavor to it. The fuel used in a grill impart a nuance of flavor. Adding aromatic wood chips such as or applewood or certain herbs such as lemongrass or fennel will impart additional flavor tones. (This cannot be done when using a broiler.)

The grill can be old fationed, using some type of charcoal, or an electric one. The best grills will allow for fairly controllable heat. To ready your grill for cooking, heat it until hot and then use a long-handled brush to scrape away any residue. Immediately before placing food on the grill, rub a wad of paper towels dipped in oil onto the grate. This will greatly reduce sticking.

Pretty much everything edible can be grilled: soft cuts of meat, poultry, game birds, seafood, fish, or vegetables. The food will grill more uniformly if you let it come to room temperature immediately before cooking. Seasoning, especially with salt, must be done just before you cook, as salt tends to draw out moisture, rendering your final product less juicy. Furthermore, foods that are naturally low in fat must be brushed with oil or butter coated with a sauce to keep them from drying out. Marinades are way to put in additional flavor to grilled foods.

To test when your grilled meat is done, it is best to use an instant-thermometer. If you don't like this method, you can insert the point of a knife to visually see if your food is done. Always bear in mind that your food carries on cooking even after you take it off the grill. Furthermore, meats will reabsorb some of their juices after they are done cooking. Make sure you let your meats rest for 5-10 minutes before you serve.

COOKING IN WATER

Simmering and poaching are both techniques that involve cooking food in liquid. With both techniques, the cooking liquid is first brought a boil and then the heat is decreased in order to reduce bubbling. Poaching should have a little less bubbling action than simmering, but it's hard to tell when something is simmering versus poaching. Some recipes require a covered cooking vessel, others open ones. As something is simmering or poaching, it is vital to skim surface regularly to remove the residue that accumulates. Fish, rice, and poultry all do great with poaching and simmering.

Only a few foods need to be boiled — noodles and potatoes being two of the most common ones. Boiling water is also used to blanch or parboil fruits vegetables before they are moved to another cooking method. Blanching involves placing the ingredients in boiling water for a short period of time and then immersing them into cold water to retain color and flavor or to make it easier to take their skins off. Ingredients that parboiled actually stay in the boiling water a small amount longer, in order to slightly tenderize them.

Another popular cooking technique involving water is steaming. With this method, the ingredients are not immersed in the water, but instead above it on a rack. The pot is covered at all times. Steaming is a very gentle cooking method and it is usually the most healthy. Steamed ingredients do not lose much of their nutrients, texture, or individual flavor. Vegetables and sticky rice do great with steaming.

ROASTING

Roasting is another fundamental cooking method used around the world. A very simple technique that requires an oven, usually with high heat. This technique can also use indirect heat from a grill to obtain similar results. Pretty much everything can be roasted: meats, fishes, vegetables, or fruits.

Roasting meat requires you to season it in some way, sometimes searing it before you place it in your oven and sometimes coating it it cooks — depending on the recipe — and always letting it rest. Resting allows the meat to reabsorb some of its juices, making your roast juicy and easier to carve. To rest your roast, you simply remove it the oven, cover it using foil, and allow it to sit.

A useful gadget to have when roasting is an ovenproof meat thermometer. This will allow you to know when your roast is done to your preference, without cutting into it. For an accurate reading, you must insert tip of the thermometer into the deepest part of the meat without touching bone, fat, or the bottom of the pan. Roasting charts commonly come with the thermometers.

HANDY TOOLS FOR THAI COOKING

KNIFE TYPES AND THEIR USES

- **CHEF'S KNIFE** — a medium-bladed knife used for chopping, cutting, mincing
- **PARING KNIFE** — a short-bladed knife (usually 2 to 4 inches) used trim fruits and vegetables
- **SLICING KNIFE** — a long-bladed knife, either smooth-edged or serrated used for cutting meats or breads

Other useful knives include: boning, utility, cleaver, and fillet.

SPECIALTY UTENSILS

If you're getting started with Thai cooking and don't wish to invest any more cash on fancy tools for the job, you will be able to get by just fine. However, if you want to make your job a little easier, you might want to add a few of these to your kitchen:

- **BLENDER** — great for making sauces and purées
- **CHINOIS** — a sieve perfect for straining stocks, sauces, and purées
- **COLANDER** — perfect for straining noodles
- **FOOD PROCESSOR** — the workhorse of the kitchen when it comes mixing, chopping, puréeing, and shredding
- **HAND BLENDER** — great for making sauces and purées right in the pot
- **MANDOLINE** — an extremely sharp utensil used for precise paper-cutting
- **MORTAR and PESTLE** — a stone container and club used to crush spices and herbs
- **RICE COOKER** — an electric gizmo that takes the guessing out of
- **WOK** — a high-sided, sloping, small-bottomed pan — the quintessential Asian utensil

BASIC FOOD SUBSTITUTIONS

If you're in a country like the USA, you might not be able to find an ingredient that a recipe calls for. When this happens, it is usually a good idea to google the ingredient, and find alternatives you can get your hands on. Below are a few of such ingredients. If you come across more, google is your friend.

THAI INGREDIENT	SUBSTITUTION
Fish sauce	Soy sauce
Cilantro	Parsley
Kaffir lime leaves	Lime peel
Lemongrass	Lemon peel
Rice vinegar	Dry sherry or white vinegar
Long beans	Green beans
Thai eggplant	Green peas
Shallots	Small onions

Homemade curry paste	Store-bought curry paste

Fish sauce is an ingredient that is used in quite a few recipes in this book, and if you can't find it in a nearby store, just buy it online from amazon.

THAI CURRY PASTES, MARINADES, AND OTHER CONCOCTIONS

ASIAN MARINADE — 1

Ingredients:

- ¼ cup fish sauce
- ¼ cup soy sauce (if possible low-sodium)
- ½ cup freshly squeezed lime juice
- 1 tablespoon curry powder
- 1 tablespoon light brown sugar
- 1 teaspoon minced garlic Crushed dried red pepper
- 2 tablespoons crispy peanut butter

Directions:

1. Mix all the ingredients in a blender or food processor and pulse until the desired smoothness is achieved.

Yield: Approximately 1¼ cups

ASIAN MARINADE — 2

Ingredients:

- ¼ cup chopped green onion
- ¼ cup soy sauce
- ¼ teaspoon ground anise
- ½ cup lime juice
- 1 tablespoon freshly grated gingerroot
- 1 tablespoon honey
- 1 teaspoon Chinese 5-spice powder

- 2 tablespoons hoisin sauce
- 2 tablespoons sesame oil
- 3 cloves garlic, minced
- 3 tablespoons chopped cilantro
- 1 cup vegetable oil

Directions:

1. Mix the lime juice, soy sauce, hoisin sauce, and honey, and blend thoroughly.
2. Slowly whisk in the vegetable and sesame oils. Put in the rest of the ingredients and mix meticulously.

Yield: Approximately 1¼ cups

This recipe has a definite Chinese influence, featuring soy sauce, hoisin sauce, 5-spice powder, and sesame oil.

BLACK BEAN PASTE

Ingredients:

- 1 medium to big onion, minced
- 1 tablespoon fish sauce
- 1 teaspoon brown sugar
- 2 cloves garlic, chopped
- 2 jalapeños, seeded and chopped
- 2 tablespoons vegetable oil
- 2 teaspoons lime juice
- 3 green onions, trimmed and cut
- 4 tablespoons canned black beans or black soy beans

Directions:

1. In a moderate-sized-sized sauté pan, heat the oil over moderate-the onions, jalapeños, garlic, and green onions, and sauté onion becomes translucent.

2. Using a slotted spoon, move the sautéed vegetables to processor or blender (set aside the oil in the sauté pan). rest of the ingredients and process for a short period of time to create a not-paste.
3. Reheat the reserved oil in the sauté pan. Move the paste and heat for five minutes, stirring continuously. If the paste seems thick, add a small amount of water.

Yield: Approximately ½ cup

CHILI TAMARIND PASTE

Ingredients:

- ½ cup dried shrimp
- 1 cup cut shallots
- 1 tablespoon fish sauce
- 1¾ cups vegetable oil, divided
- 12 small Thai chilies or
- 3 tablespoons brown sugar
- 3 tablespoons Tamarind Concentrate (Page 20)
- 6 serrano chilies
- 1 cup garlic

Directions:

1. Put the dried shrimp in a small container. Cover the shrimp stir for a short period of time, and drain; set aside.
2. Pour 1½ cups of the vegetable oil in a moderate-sized deep cooking pan. the oil to roughly 360 degrees on moderate to high heat.
3. Put in the garlic and fry until a golden-brown colour is achieved. Using a slotted move the garlic to a container lined using paper towels.
4. Put in the shallots to the deep cooking pan and fry for two to three minutes; the shallots to the container with the garlic.
5. Fry the reserved shrimp in the deep cooking pan for a couple of minutes; the container.
6. Fry the chilies until they become brittle, approximately half a minute; them to the container. (Allow oil to cool completely discarding.)

7. Mix the fried ingredients, the rest of the oil, and the a food processor; process to make a smooth paste.
8. Put the paste in a small deep cooking pan on moderate heat. Put in the sugar and fish sauce, and cook, stirring once in a while, for approximately five minutes.
9. Allow the paste to return to room temperature before placing in an airtight container.

Yield: Approximately 3 cups

CHILI VINEGAR

Ingredients:

- ½ cup white vinegar
- 2 teaspoons fish sauce
- 3 serrano chilies, seeded and finely cut

Directions:

1. Put all of the ingredients in a container.
2. Allow to sit minimum twenty minutes to allow the flavors to develop.

Yield: Approximately ½ cup

COCONUT MARINADE

Ingredients:

- ¼–½ teaspoon red chili pepper flakes
- 1 tablespoon grated lime zest
- 1 tablespoon minced fresh ginger
- 2 tablespoons shredded, unsweetened coconut
- 2 teaspoons sugar
- 3 tablespoons lime juice
- 3 tablespoons rice wine vinegar
- teaspoon curry powder

Directions:

1. Warm the vinegar using low heat. Put in the coconut and ginger to become tender.
2. Turn off the heat and mix in the rest of the ingredients.

Yield: Approximately ½ cup

GREEN CURRY PASTE — 1

Ingredients:

- ¼ cup vegetable oil
- ½ cup chopped cilantro
- ½ teaspoon ground cloves
- ½ teaspoon shrimp paste
- 1 (1½-inch) piece gingerroot, peeled and chopped
- 1 stalk lemongrass, tough outer leaves removed, inner soft portion chopped
- 1 teaspoon black pepper
- 1 teaspoon ground cumin
- 1 teaspoon salt
- 10 green serrano chilies
- 2 teaspoons grated lime zest
- 2 teaspoons ground coriander
- 2 teaspoons ground nutmeg
- 3 shallots, crudely chopped
- 5 cloves garlic

Directions:

1. Put the first 6 ingredients in a food processor and process mixed. Put in the rest of the ingredients, apart from the vegetable process until the desired smoothness is achieved.
2. Slowly put in the oil until a thick paste May be placed in the fridge up to 4 weeks.

Yield: 1 cup

GREEN CURRY PASTE — 2

Ingredients:

- 1 (1-inch) piece ginger, peeled and chopped
- 1 medium onion, chopped
- 1 teaspoon salt
- 1 teaspoon shrimp paste
- 2 green bell peppers, seeded and chopped
- 2 tablespoons vegetable oil
- 2 teaspoons chopped lemongrass
- 2 teaspoons cumin seeds, toasted
- 2–4 green jalapeño chilies, seeded and chopped
- 3 cloves garlic, chopped
- 3 tablespoons coriander seeds, toasted
- 3 teaspoons water
- 4 tablespoons chopped cilantro
- 4 tablespoons Tamarind Concentrate (Page 20)

Directions:

1. Put all the ingredients in a food processor and pulse until the desired smoothness is achieved. Move to a small deep cooking pan and bring to a simmer on moderate to low heat. Decrease the heat to low and cook, stirring regularly, for five minutes.
2. Mix in 1 cup of water and bring the mixture to its boiling point. Decrease the heat, cover, and simmer for half an hour

Yield: Approximately 1 cup

LEMON CHILI VINEGAR

Ingredients:

- 1 quart white wine vinegar Peel of 4 limes
- 8–10 serrano chilies

Directions:

1. Mix all the ingredients in a moderate-sized deep cooking pan and bring to a simmer on moderate heat.
2. Decrease the heat and simmer for about ten minutes.
3. Cool to room temperature, then strain.

Yield: Approximately 1 quart

LEMONGRASS MARINADE

Ingredients:

- ¼ tablespoon soy sauce
- 1 cup extra-virgin olive oil
- 1 jalapeño chili pepper, seeded and chopped
- 1 tablespoon fish sauce
- 2 cloves garlic, minced
- 2 stalks lemongrass, trimmed and smashed
- 2 tablespoons chopped cilantro
- 2 tablespoons lime juice

Directions:

1. Pour the olive oil into a pan and heat until warm.
2. Put in the lemongrass and garlic, and cook for a minute. Turn off the heat and let cool completely.
3. Mix in the rest of the ingredients.

Yield: Approximately 1 cups

MALAYSIAN MARINADE

Ingredients:

- ¼ cup chopped cilantro

- ¼ cup soy sauce
- ¼ cup vegetable oil
- ½ teaspoon coriander
- ½ teaspoon ground cumin
- 1 green onion, trimmed and thinly cut
- 1 teaspoon grated lime zest
- 2 tablespoons grated gingerroot
- 2 tablespoons honey
- 3 tablespoons lime juice

Directions:

1. Mix the honey, lime juice, lime zest, and soy sauce in a small container.
2. Slowly whisk in the oil.
3. Mix in the rest of the ingredients.

Yield: Approximately 1 cup

MINTY TAMARIND PASTE

Ingredients:

- ¼ cup peanuts
- ½ cup Tamarind Concentrate (Page 20)
- 1 bunch cilantro leaves
- 1 bunch mint leaves
- 4–5 Thai bird peppers or 2 serrano chilies, seeded and chopped

Directions:

1. Put all the ingredients in a food processor and pulse to make a paste.

Yield: Approximately 2 cups

NORTHERN (OR JUNGLE) CURRY PASTE

Ingredients:

- ¼ cup chopped arugula
- ¼ cup chopped chives
- ½ cup chopped mint
- 1 (3-inch) piece ginger, peeled and chopped
- 1 cup chopped basil
- 1 stalk lemongrass, tough outer leaves removed and discarded, inner core minced
- 1 tablespoon shrimp paste
- 12 serrano chilies, seeded and chopped
- 2 tablespoons vegetable oil
- 4 shallots, chopped
- 6–8 Thai bird chilies, seeded and chopped

Directions:

1. In a moderate-sized-sized sauté pan, heat the oil on medium. Put in shrimp paste, lemongrass, ginger, and shallots, and sauté until shallots start to turn translucent and the mixture is very aromatic.
2. Move the mixture to a food processor and pulse until adding 1 or 2 tablespoons of water to help with the grinding.
3. Put in the rest of the ingredients and more water if required to pulse until crudely mixed.

Yield: Approximately 2 cups

RED CURRY PASTE — 1

Ingredients:

- 1 (½-inch) piece ginger, finely chopped
- 1 medium onion, chopped
- 1 stalk lemongrass, outer leaves removed and discarded, inner core finely chopped
- 1 teaspoon salt
- 2 garlic cloves, chopped
- 2 tablespoons Tamarind Concentrate (Page 20)

- 2 teaspoons cumin seeds, toasted
- 2 teaspoons paprika
- 3 kaffir lime leaves or the peel of 1 lime, chopped
- 3 tablespoons coriander seeds, toasted
- 3 tablespoons vegetable oil
- 4 tablespoons water
- 6–8 red serrano chilies, seeded and chopped

Directions:

1. Put all the ingredients in a food processor and pulse until super smooth.
2. Move to a small deep cooking pan and bring to a simmer on moderate to low heat. Decrease the heat to low and cook, stirring regularly, for five minutes.
3. Mix in 1 cup of water and bring the mixture to its boiling point. Decrease the heat, cover, and simmer thirty minutes.

Yield: Approximately ½ cup

RED CURRY PASTE— 2

Ingredients:

- 1 (2-inch) piece ginger, peeled and thoroughly minced
- 1 small onion, chopped
- 2 cloves garlic, minced
- 2 stalks lemongrass, tough outer leaves removed and discarded, inner core thoroughly minced
- 2 tablespoons ground turmeric
- 3 big dried red California chilies, seeded and chopped
- 5 dried Thai bird or similar chilies, seeded and chopped

Directions:

1. Put the chilies in a container and cover them with hot water. Allow to stand for minimum 30 minutes. Drain the chilies, saving for later 1 cup of the soaking liquid.

2. Put all the ingredients and 2–3 tablespoons of the soaking liquid in a food processor. Process to make a thick, smooth paste. Put in additional liquid if required.

Yield: Approximately 1 cup

SHREDDED FRESH COCONUT

Ingredients:

- 1 heavy coconut, with liquid

Directions:

1. Preheat your oven to 400 degrees.
2. Pierce the eye of the coconut using a metal skewer or screwdriver and drain the coconut water (reserve it for later use if you prefer).
3. Bake the coconut for fifteen minutes, then remove and allow to cool.
4. When the coconut is sufficiently cool to handle, use a hammer to break the shell. Using the tip of a knife, cautiously pull the flesh from the shell. Remove any remaining brown membrane with a vegetable peeler.
5. Shred the coconut using a 4-sided grater. Fresh coconut will keep in your fridge for maximum one week.

Yield: Approximately 1 cup

SOUTHERN (OR MASSAMAN) CURRY PASTE

Ingredients:

- ¼ teaspoon ground cinnamon
- ¼ teaspoon whole black peppercorns
- ½ teaspoon cardamom seeds, toasted
- 1 (1-inch) piece ginger, peeled and minced
- 1 stalk lemongrass, tough outer leaves removed and discarded, inner core finely chopped
- 1 teaspoon lime peel
- 1 teaspoon salt

- 1 teaspoon shrimp paste (not necessary)
- 2 tablespoons coriander seeds, toasted
- 2 tablespoons vegetable oil
- 2 teaspoons brown sugar
- 2 teaspoons cumin seeds, toasted
- 2 whole cloves
- 3 tablespoons Tamarind Concentrate (Page 20)
- 3 tablespoons water
- 6–8 big dried red chilies (often called California chilies), soaked in hot water for five minutes and drained

Directions:

1. Put all ingredients in a food processor and pulse until the desired smoothness is achieved.
2. Move to a small deep cooking pan and bring to a simmer on moderate to low heat. Decrease the heat to low and cook, stirring regularly, for five minutes.
3. Mix in 1 cup of water and bring the mixture to its boiling point. Decrease the heat, cover, and simmer thirty minutes.

Yield: Approximately 1 cup

TAMARIND CONCENTRATE

Ingredients:

- 1 cup warm water
- 2 ounces seedless tamarind pulp (sold in Asian markets)

Directions:

1. Put the tamarind pulp and water in a small container for about twenty minutes or until the pulp is tender.
2. Break the pulp apart using the backside of a spoon and stir until blended.
3. Pour the mixture through a fine-mesh sieve, pushing the tender pulp through the strainer. Discard any fibrous pulp remaining in the strainer.

Yield: Approximately 1 cup

TAMARIND MARINADE

Ingredients:

- ¼ cup fresh lime juice
- ¼ cup toasted, unsweetened coconut
- ¼ cup vegetable oil
- ½ cup chopped cilantro leaves
- 1 shallot, chopped
- 1 tablespoon brown sugar
- 1 tablespoon diced fresh gingerroot
- 1 tablespoon soy sauce
- 1½ cups Tamarind Concentrate (Page 20)
- 2 garlic cloves, minced
- 4 pieces lime peel (roughly ½-inch by two-inches)

Directions:

1. Mix the tamarind and lime peel in a small deep cooking pan and bring to a simmer; cook for five minutes.
2. Turn off the heat and cool completely. Mix in the rest of the ingredients.

Yield: Approximately 2 cups

THAI GRILLING RUB

Ingredients:

- 1 teaspoon dried lime peel
- 1 teaspoon freshly ground black pepper
- 1 teaspoon ground ginger
- 4 teaspoons salt

Directions:

1. Mix all the ingredients and mix meticulously. Store in an airtight container.
2. To use, wash the meat of your choice under cool water and pat dry; drizzle the meat with the spice mixture (to taste) and rub it in together with some olive oil, then grill or broil to your preference.

Yield: Approximately

THAI MARINADE — 1

Ingredients:

- ¼ cup chopped cilantro
- ¼ cup fresh lime juice
- ¼ teaspoon hot pepper flakes
- ½ cup sesame oil
- 1 big stalk lemongrass, crushed
- 1 tablespoon brown sugar
- 2 tablespoons chopped peanuts
- 2 tablespoons fish sauce
- 3 cloves garlic, minced

Directions:

1. Mix the fish sauce and lime juice in a small container.
2. Slowly whisk in the sesame oil, then mix in rest of the ingredients.

Yield: Approximately 1 cup

THAI MARINADE — 2

Ingredients:

- ¼ cup chopped basil leaves
- ¼ cup chopped mint leaves

- ¼ cup peanut oil
- ½ cup rice wine
- 1 small onion, chopped
- 1 tablespoon chopped gingerroot
- 1 tablespoon sweet soy sauce
- 2 tablespoons chopped lemongrass
- 3 cloves garlic, minced
- 3 tablespoons fish sauce

Directions:

1. Mix the fish sauce, sweet soy sauce, and the rice wine in a small container.
2. Slowly whisk in the peanut oil, then mix in rest of the ingredients.

Yield: Approximately 1½ cups

THAI MARINADE — 3

Ingredients:

- ¼ cup chopped cilantro leaves
- ¼ cup lime juice
- ½ cup Red Curry Paste (Page 17)
- 1 (12-ounce) can coconut milk
- 1 stalk lemongrass, roughly chopped
- 1 tablespoon sweet soy sauce
- 1 teaspoon fresh gingerroot, chopped
- 2 tablespoons fish sauce
- 6 kaffir lime leaves, finely cut

Directions:

1. Mix the coconut milk, curry paste, lemongrass, and kaffir leaves in a small deep cooking pan; bring to a simmer on moderate heat.
2. Decrease the heat and carry on simmering for fifteen minutes.

3. Turn off the heat and let cool to room temperature.
4. Mix in all the rest of the ingredients.

Yield: Approximately 2 cups

THAI VINEGAR MARINADE

Ingredients:

- ¼ cup chopped lemongrass
- 1 tablespoon fresh grated gingerroot
- 1 tablespoon sugar
- 2–3 tablespoons vegetable oil
- 3 tablespoons chopped green onion
- 3½ cups rice wine vinegar
- 4 cloves garlic, minced
- 6 dried red chilies, seeded and crumbled

Directions:

1. Put the garlic, chilies, green onions, and ginger in a food processor or blender and process to make a paste.
2. Heat the oil in a wok or frying pan, put in the paste, and stir-fry for four to five minutes. Turn off the heat and allow the mixture to cool completely.
3. In a small deep cooking pan, bring the vinegar to its boiling point. Put in the sugar and the lemongrass; decrease the heat and simmer for about twenty minutes.
4. Mix in the reserved paste.

Yield: Approximately 3 cups

YELLOW BEAN SAUCE

Ingredients:

- 1 (½-inch) piece ginger, peeled and chopped

- 1 medium to big onion, minced
- 1 teaspoon ground coriander
- 2 serrano chilies, seeded and chopped
- 2 tablespoons lime juice
- 2 tablespoons vegetable oil
- 2 tablespoons water
- 4 tablespoons fermented yellow beans (fermented soy beans)

Directions:

1. In a moderate-sized-sized sauté pan, heat the oil on moderate heat. Put in the onion and chilies, and sauté until the onion becomes translucent. Mix in the ginger and coriander, and carry on cooking for half a minute.
2. Put in the beans, lime juice, and water, and simmer using low heat for about ten minutes.
3. Move the mixture to a blender and process until the desired smoothness is achieved.

Yield: Approximately 1 cup

DIPPING SAUCES, SALSAS, AND VINAIGRETTES

5-MINUTE DIPPING SAUCE

Ingredients:

- ½ teaspoon dried red pepper flakes
- 1 tablespoon fish sauce
- 1 tablespoon lime juice
- 1 teaspoon minced fresh ginger
- 1 teaspoon sugar

Directions:

1. In a small container, dissolve the sugar in 1 tablespoon of water.
2. Mix in the rest of the ingredients; tweak seasonings if required. Serve at room temperature.

Yield: Approximately 4 tablespoons

BANANA, TAMARIND, AND MINT SALSA

Ingredients:

- ¼ cup Tamarind Concentrate (Page 20)
- 1 roasted red jalapeño, seeded and chopped
- 1 tablespoon chopped fresh mint
- 1 tablespoon lime juice
- 1 teaspoon brown sugar
- 4 ripe bananas, peeled and finely diced

Directions:

1. Lightly fold all the ingredients together.

Yield: Approximately 2 cups

This unique salsa goes perfectly with roasted or grilled poultry or game.

GINGER-LEMONGRASS VINAIGRETTE

Ingredients:

- ¼ cup grated fresh gingerroot
- 1 quart rice wine vinegar
- 2 stalks lemongrass, outer leaves removed and discarded, inner core slightly mashed

Directions:

1. Mix all the ingredients in a nonreactive pot and simmer using low heat for half an hour.
2. Turn off the heat and allow it to stand overnight. Strain before you serve.

Yield: Approximately 1 quart

JALAPEÑO-LIME VINAIGRETTE

Ingredients:

- 1 cup vegetable or canola oil
- 1 jalapeño, seeded and chopped
- 1 tablespoon sugar
- 1 cup lime juice
- Salt and pepper to taste

Directions:

1. Put the jalapeño, lime juice, sugar, and salt and pepper in a food processor; blend for a minute.
2. While continuing to blend, slowly put in the oil; blend for half a minute or until well blended.

Yield: Approximately 1 cups

MANGO-CUCUMBER SALSA

Ingredients:

- ¼ cup cut green onion
- ¼ cup orange juice
- 1 firm, ripe mango, peeled, seeded, and slice into ¼-inch dice
- 1 medium cucumber, seeded and slice into ¼-inch dice
- 1 teaspoon vegetable oil
- 2 teaspoons lime juice
- Salt and pepper to taste

Directions:

1. Mix all the ingredients in a small container.

Yield: Approximately 2 cups

MANGO-PINEAPPLE SALSA

Ingredients:

- ¼ cup snipped chives
- ½ cup diced red onion
- 1 cup diced pineapple
- 1 cup mango pieces
- 1 cup seeded and chopped tomato
- 1 serrano chili, seeded and chopped
- 2 tablespoons lime juice
- 2 tablespoons vegetable oil Salt and pepper to taste
- 3 tablespoons chopped cilantro

Directions:

1. Mix all the ingredients in a small container.
2. Cover and place in your fridge for minimum 2 hours before you serve.

Yield: Approximately 4 cups

MINT-CILANTRO "CHUTNEY"

Ingredients:

- ½ teaspoon minced honey
- ¾ cup packed cilantro
- ¾ cup packed mint leaves
- 2 teaspoons honey
- 3 tablespoons sour cream
- 1 cup unsalted peanuts, toasted
- Salt and pepper to taste

Directions:

1. Put the peanuts in a food processor and finely grind.
2. Put in the rest of the ingredients to the processor and blend until well blended.

Yield: Approximately 2 cups

MINTY DIPPING SAUCE

Ingredients:

- ¼ cup chopped mint leaves
- ¼ cup lime juice
- 1 serrano chili, seeded and diced
- 1 tablespoon grated lime zest
- 2 cloves garlic, minced
- 2 tablespoons fish sauce

Directions:

1. Put all the ingredients in a blender and process until the desired smoothness is achieved.
2. Serve with a variety of grilled, skewered meats and raw or blanched vegetables.

Yield: Approximately 1 cup

PEANUT DIPPING SAUCE — 1

Ingredients:

- ¼ cup chicken or vegetable stock
- ¼ cup heavy cream
- ¼ cup lemon juice
- 1 teaspoon grated gingerroot
- 1½ cups coconut milk
- 2 tablespoons brown sugar
- 2 tablespoons soy sauce
- 3–4 dashes (or to taste) Tabasco
- 4 cloves garlic, pressed
- 1 cup crispy peanut butter

Directions:

1. Mix the peanut butter, coconut milk, lemon juice, soy sauce, brown sugar, ginger, garlic, and Tabasco in a small deep cooking pan on moderate heat. Cook while stirring continuously, until the sauce has the consistency of heavy cream, approximately fifteen minutes.
2. Move the mixture to a blender and purée for a short period of time.
3. Put in the stock and cream, and blend until the desired smoothness is achieved.

Yield: Approximately 2 cups

PEANUT DIPPING SAUCE — 2

Ingredients:

- ¼ cup fresh lime juice
- ¼ cup half-and-half or heavy cream
- ¼ cup low-sodium beef broth

- 1 teaspoon grated gingerroot
- 1½ cups unsweetened canned coconut milk
- 2 tablespoons brown sugar
- 2 tablespoons soy sauce
- 2 teaspoons minced garlic Ground cayenne or crushed red pepper flakes to taste
- 1 cup crispy peanut butter

Directions:

1. In a moderate-sized-sized deep cooking pan, mix the peanut butter, coconut milk, lime juice, soy sauce, brown sugar, ginger, garlic, and cayenne.
2. Stirring continuously, cook on moderate heat until the sauce thickens, approximately fifteen minutes.
3. Take away the sauce from the heat and put in the beef broth and cream. Using a hand mixer, blend until the desired smoothness is achieved. Heat for a short period of time just prior to serving.

Yield: Approximately 2 cups

PEANUT DIPPING SAUCE — 3

Ingredients:

- ½ cup smooth peanut butter
- 1 cup canned coconut milk
- 1 tablespoon fish sauce
- 1 teaspoon fresh lemon juice
- 1 teaspoon Tabasco
- 2 tablespoons fresh lime juice
- 2 teaspoons light brown sugar
- 2 teaspoons soy sauce
- 3 shallots

Directions:

1. Roast the shallots in an oven preheated to 325 degrees for approximately five minutes or until tender. Allow them to cool to roughly room temperature.
2. Put all ingredients in a blender or food processor and pulse until the desired smoothness is achieved.

Yield: Approximately 2 cups

PEANUT PESTO

Ingredients:

- ¼ cup honey
- ¼ teaspoon (or to taste) red pepper flakes
- ½ cup sesame oil
- ½ cup soy sauce
- 1 cup unsalted roasted peanuts
- 2–3 cloves garlic, minced
- 1 cup water

Directions:

1. Put the peanuts in a food processor fitted using a metal blade; pulse until fine.
2. While continuing to blend, put in the rest of the ingredients one by one through the feed tube until well mixed.

Yield: Approximately 2 cups

QUICK HOT DIPPING SAUCE

Ingredients:

- ½ cup white vinegar
- 1 loaded tablespoon prepared chili-garlic sauce

Directions:

1. Mix the 2 ingredients before you serve.

Yield: Approximately ½ cup

SPICY THAI DRESSING

Ingredients:

- 1 fresh red cayenne pepper or
- 1 tablespoon plus 1 teaspoon rice wine vinegar
- 1 tablespoon sesame oil
- 1 teaspoon grated gingerroot
- 1 teaspoon sugar
- 2 cloves garlic
- 2 tablespoons soy sauce
- 2 Thai peppers, stemmed, seeded, and slice into pieces
- 3 tablespoons water

Directions:

1. Put all the ingredients in a blender and process until the desired smoothness is achieved.

Yield: Approximately 1 cup

SWEET-AND-SOUR DIPPING SAUCE

Ingredients:

- ½ cup white vinegar
- ½ teaspoon salt
- 1 cup sugar
- 1 loaded tablespoon prepared chili-garlic sauce

Directions:

1. Mix the vinegar, sugar, and salt in a small deep cooking pan on moderate to high heat; bring to its boiling point, reduce to a simmer, and cook for eight to ten minutes, stirring once in a while.

2. Mix in the chili sauce and turn off the heat. Allow to cool to room temperature before you serve.

Yield: Approximately 1½ cups

THAI-STYLE PLUM DIPPING SAUCE

Ingredients:

- 2 tablespoons honey Tabasco to taste
- 1 cup plum preserves
- 1 cup water
- 1 cup white vinegar

Directions:

1. Put all the ingredients apart from the Tabasco in a food processor or blender, and process until the desired smoothness is achieved.
2. Move the mixture to a small deep cooking pan and bring to its boiling point on moderate heat; decrease the heat and simmer until thick, approximately twelve to fifteen minutes.
3. Allow to cool completely, then mix in the Tabasco.

Yield: Approximately 2 cups

APPETIZERS

3-FLAVOR RICE STICKS

Ingredients:

- 1 pound rice sticks, broken into 3-inch segments
- Cayenne pepper to taste
- Curry powder to taste
- Salt to taste
- Vegetable oil for frying

Directions:

1. Pour 2 to 3 inches of vegetable oil into a big frying pan and heat to 350 degrees. Fry the rice sticks in batches (ensuring not to overcrowd the pan), turning them swiftly as they puff up. After they stop crackling in the oil, move the puffed sticks to paper towels to drain.
2. While the rice sticks are still hot, drizzle salt on 1 batch; drizzle a second batch with curry powder; and a third batch with cayenne pepper to taste.

Yield: Servings 4–6

BASIL AND SHRIMP WEDGES

Ingredients:

- ½ cup julienned basil
- ½ pound cooked salad shrimp
- 1 green onion, trimmed and thinly cut
- 1 teaspoon fish sauce
- 1½ teaspoons vegetable oil, divided
- 2 tablespoons water
- 4 eggs

- Salt and pepper to taste

Directions:

1. Put 1 teaspoon of the vegetable oil in a sauté pan on moderate heat. Put in the shrimp and green onion, and sauté until the shrimp are warmed through, roughly two minutes. Put in the basil and fish sauce and cook for 1 more minute. Set aside.
2. In a big container, whisk together the eggs, water, and salt and pepper, then mix in the shrimp mixture.
3. Put the remaining ½ teaspoon of vegetable oil in an omelet pan on moderate heat. Put in the egg mixture and cook until the omelet starts to brown. Turn over the omelet and carry on cooking until set.
4. To serve, slide the omelet onto a serving plate and cut it into wedges. Serve with a Thai dipping sauce of your choice.

Yield: Servings 4–6 as an appetizer or 2 as a brunch item

CHICKEN, SHRIMP, AND BEEF SATAY

CHICKEN

- 1 recipe Peanut Dipping Sauce
- 1 recipe Thai Marinade (Page 22)
- 3 whole boneless, skinless chicken breasts, cut into lengthy strips about ½-inch wide

Directions:

1. Thread the chicken strips onto presoaked bamboo skewers or onto metal skewers. Put the skewers in a flat pan and cover with marinade. Marinate the chicken in your fridge overnight.
2. Cook the skewers on the grill or under the broiler, coating and turning them until they are thoroughly cooked, approximately six to eight minutes.
3. Serve with the peanut sauce for dipping.

SHRIMP

- 1 recipe Peanut Dipping Sauce
- 1 recipe Thai Marinade (Page 22)
- 24 big shrimp, shelled and deveined

Directions:

1. Thread the shrimp onto presoaked bamboo skewers or onto metal skewers (about 3 shrimp per skewer). Put the skewers in a flat pan and cover with marinade. Marinate the shrimp for minimum fifteen minutes, but no longer than an hour.
2. Cook the skewers on the grill or under the broiler, coating and turning them frequently until just opaque, approximately three to four minutes.
3. Serve with the peanut sauce for dipping.

Yield: 4–6 chicken skewers or 6–8 shrimp or beef skewers

BEEF

- 1 recipe Thai Marinade (Page 22)
- 1 recipe Peanut Dipping Sauce
- 1-1½ pounds sirloin steak, fat and sinew removed, cut into ½-inch-wide strips

Directions:

1. Thread the beef strips onto presoaked bamboo skewers or onto metal skewers. Put the skewers in a flat pan and cover with marinade. Marinate the beef in your fridge overnight.
2. Cook the skewers on the grill or under the broiler, coating and turning them frequently until done to your preference, approximately six to eight minutes for medium.
3. Serve with the peanut sauce for dipping.

CHINESE-STYLE DUMPLINGS

Ingredients:

- ¼ cup sticky rice flour
- ¼ cup tapioca flour
- ½ cup water

- 1 cup rice flour
- 1 tablespoon soy sauce
- 1 teaspoon vegetable oil
- 2 cups chives, cut into ½–inch lengths

Directions:

1. In a moderate-sized-sized deep cooking pan, mix together the sticky rice flour, the rice flour, and the water. Turn the heat to moderate and cook, stirring continuously until the mixture has the consistency of glue. (If the mixture becomes too sticky, decrease the heat to low.) Take away the batter from the heat and swiftly mix in the tapioca flour. Set aside to cool completely.
2. In the meantime, put in the vegetable oil to a frying pan big enough to easily hold the chives, and heat on high. Put in the chives and the soy sauce. Stir-fry the chives just until they wilt. Be careful not to let the chives cook excessively. Turn off the heat and save for later.
3. Once the dough has reached room temperature, check its consistency. If it is too sticky to work with, add a little extra tapioca flour.
4. To make the dumplings, roll the batter into balls an inch in diameter. Using your fingers, flatten each ball into a disk approximately four inches across. Ladle approximately 1 tablespoon of the chives into the middle of each disk. Fold the disk in half and pinch the edges together to make a halfmoon-shaped packet.
5. Put the dumplings in a prepared steamer for five to 8 minutes or until the dough is cooked. Serve with a spicy dipping sauce of your choice.

Yield: 15–20 dumplings

COLD SESAME NOODLES

Ingredients:

- ¼ cup creamy peanut butter or tahini
- ¼–½ teaspoon dried red pepper flakes
- 1 pound angel hair pasta
- 1 tablespoon grated ginger

- 1–2 green onions, trimmed and thinly cut (not necessary)
- 2 tablespoons rice vinegar
- 2 tablespoons sesame oil

Directions:

1. Cook the pasta in accordance with package directions. Wash under cold water, then set aside.
2. Vigorously whisk together the rest of the ingredients; pour over pasta, tossing to coat.
3. Decorate using green onion if you wish.

Yield: Servings 2–4

CRAB SPRING ROLLS

Ingredients:

- ¼–½ teaspoon grated lime peel
- 1 pound crabmeat, picked over to remove any shells, and shredded
- 1 tablespoon mayonnaise
- 2 egg yolks, lightly beaten
- Canola oil for deep frying
- fifteen small, soft Boston lettuce leaves
- fifteen spring roll or egg roll wrappers
- Mint leaves
- Parsley leaves

Directions:

1. In a small container, combine the crabmeat with the mayonnaise and lime peel.
2. Put 1 tablespoon of the crabmeat mixture in the middle of 1 spring roll wrapper. Fold a pointed end of the wrapper over the crabmeat, then fold the opposite point over the top of the folded point. Brush a small amount of the egg yolk over the top of the uncovered wrapper, then fold the bottom point over the crabmeat and roll to make a tight packet; set aside. Repeat with the rest of the crabmeat and wrappers.

3. Heat the oil to 365 degrees in a frying pan or deep fryer. Deep-fry the rolls three to 4 at a time for a couple of minutes or so, until they are a golden brown; drain using paper towels.

4. To serve, wrap each spring roll in a wrapper with a single piece of lettuce, and a drizzling of mint and parsley. Serve with a dipping sauce of your choice.

Yield: fifteen rolls

CRISPY MUSSEL PANCAKES

Ingredients:

- ¼ cup all-purpose flour
- ¼ teaspoon salt
- ½ cup tapioca flour
- ¾ cup water
- 1 cup shelled mussels (approximately 1 pound before shelling)
- 1 teaspoon baking powder
- 2 cups bean sprouts
- 2 tablespoons chopped cilantro, plus extra for decoration
- Salt and ground pepper to taste

Directions:

1. To prepare the mussels, wash them swiftly using cool running water. Debeard the mussels by pulling out the brown membrane that is sometimes still attached. Discard any mussels that are already open. Fill a big frying pan with ½ to an inch of water. Bring the water to its boiling point, then put in the mussels, cover, and allow to steam approximately four minutes or until the mussels have opened, shaking the pan every so frequently. Drain the mussels through a colander. Allow to cool to room temperature and then use a small fork to pull the meat from the shell; set aside using paper towels.

2. In a moderate-sized-sized mixing container, mix together the flours, the salt, and the baking powder. Whisk in the water to make a thin batter.

3. Preheat your oven to 200 degrees. In a large, heavy-bottomed frying pan, heat the vegetable oil on moderate to high heat. Pour half of the batter into the frying pan and

top with half of the mussels. Cook until the batter has set and turned golden, approximately 2 minutes. Cautiously flip the pancake over and carry on cooking until golden. Take away the pancake to a baking sheet lined with some foil and place it in your oven to keep warm. Repeat to make a second pancake with the rest of the batter and mussels.

4. Put in 1 teaspoon of vegetable oil to the frying pan if it is dry, and raise the heat to high. Put in the bean sprouts, drizzle with salt and ground pepper to taste, and stir-fry swiftly just to heat through, approximately half a minute.

5. To serve, place each pancake in the middle of a plate. Top with the bean sprouts, some cilantro, and a grind of fresh pepper. Serve with a sweet-and-sour sauce of your choice.

Yield: Servings 2–4

CURRIED FISH CAKES

Ingredients:

-   ¼ cup chopped garlic
-   ¼ cup chopped lemongrass, inner portion only
-   ¼ cup chopped shallots
-   ½ pound French beans, trimmed and finely chopped
-   ½ tablespoon salt
-   ½ teaspoon peppercorns
-   1 egg, beaten
-   1 pound boneless whitefish steak, minced
-   1 tablespoon chopped ginger
-   1 tablespoon shrimp paste
-   1 teaspoon grated lime peel
-   5–10 dried chilies, seeded, soaked, and shredded
-   Vegetable oil for frying

Directions:

1. Put the shallots, garlic, lemongrass, ginger, peppercorns, lime peel, shrimp paste, chilies, and salt in a food processor or blender and process to make a smooth paste.
2. Put in the fish to the food processor and pulse until well blended with the spice paste. Put in the beaten egg and mix one more time. Move the fish mixture to a big mixing container and mix in the green beans.
3. Using roughly 1 tablespoon of fish mixture, form a flat, round cake; repeat until all of the mixture is used.
4. Heat roughly to ¼ inch of vegetable oil to 350 degrees on moderate to high heat in a frying pan or deep fryer; fry the fish cakes until golden.

Serve with a dipping sauce of your choice.

Yield: 15–20 small cakes

FRIED TOFU WITH DIPPING SAUCES

Ingredients:

- 1 package of tofu, cut into bite-sized cubes
- Dipping sauces of your choice
- Vegetable oil for frying

Directions:

1. Put in approximately two to three inches of vegetable oil to a deep fryer or wok. Heat the oil on medium until it reaches about 350 degrees. Cautiously add some of the tofu pieces, ensuring not to overcrowd them; fry until a golden-brown colour is achieved, turning continuously. Move the fried tofu to paper towels to drain as each batch is cooked.
2. Serve the tofu with a choice of dipping sauces, such as Sweet-and- Sour, Peanut, and Minty Dipping Sauce .

Yield: Servings 2–4

FRIED WON TONS

Ingredients:

- ½ cup chopped white mushrooms
- ½ pound ground pork
- 1 clove garlic, minced
- 1 tablespoon soy sauce
- 2 tablespoons minced cilantro
- 25 won ton skins
- Pinch white pepper
- Vegetable oil for frying

Directions:

1. In a moderate-sized-sized mixing container, meticulously mix the garlic, cilantro, soy sauce, mushrooms, white pepper, and ground pork.
2. To make the won tons, place roughly ½ teaspoon of the filling in the center of a won ton skin. Fold the won ton from corner to corner, making a triangle. Push the edges together to secure closed. Repeat with the rest of the skins and filling.
3. Put in approximately two to three inches of vegetable oil to a deep fryer or wok. Heat the oil on medium until it reaches about 350 degrees. Cautiously add the won tons, 2 or 3 at a time. Fry until they become golden brown, turning them continuously. Move the cooked won tons to drain using paper towels as they are done.
4. Serve the won tons with either sweet-and-sour sauce or the sauce of your choice.

Yield: Approximately 25 won tons

MEE KROB

Ingredients:

- ½ cup dried shrimp
- ½ pound thin rice stick noodles, broken into handfuls
- 1 cup bean sprouts
- 1 tablespoon Tamarind Concentrate (Page 20)
- 10 small lime wedges
- 2 eggs, beaten

- 2–3 drops red food coloring
- 5 tablespoons sugar
- 1 cup honey
- 1 cup rice or white vinegar
- Vegetable oil for deep-frying

Directions:

1. Mix the honey, vinegar, sugar, food coloring, and tamarind in a moderate-sized deep cooking pan. Bring the mixture to its boiling point on moderate heat, stirring once in a while. Decrease the heat and simmer for two to three minutes or until the mixture starts to thicken; turn off the heat and save for later.
2. Bring about 3 inches of vegetable oil to 360 degrees in a deep fryer or frying pan. Drop a single layer of the rice stick noodles into the hot oil, ensuring to leave enough room for them to cook uniformly. Turn the noodles using a slotted spoon the moment they start to puff up. Once the noodles are golden, remove them to paper towels to drain. Repeat until all of the noodles are cooked.
3. Put in the dried shrimp to the oil and cook for 45 seconds or so. Remove to paper towels.
4. Pour out all but a thin coat of the oil from the frying pan. Put in the beaten eggs and stir-fry them swiftly, shirring them into lengthy strips. Once they are cooked, remove them to paper towels.
5. Bring the sauce back to its boiling point. Mix in the shrimp and continue to boil for a couple of minutes.
6. Put about of the noodles on a serving platter and spoon about of the sauce over the top; lightly toss to coat the noodles uniformly being cautious not to crush the noodles. Repeat until all of the noodles are coated in sauce.
7. To serve, mound the noodles, put the egg strips over them, and top with the bean sprouts. Pass the lime wedges.

Yield: Servings 4–6

OMELET "EGG ROLLS"

Ingredients:

For the filling:

- ½ pound ground pork or chicken
- ½ teaspoon sugar
- 1 cup shredded Chinese cabbage
- 1 tablespoon fish sauce
- 1 tablespoon minced cilantro
- 1 teaspoon vegetable oil
- 2 green onions, trimmed and thinly cut

For the omelets:

- 1 tablespoon soy or fish sauce
- 1 teaspoon vegetable oil
- 6 tablespoons water
- 8 eggs
- Bibb lettuce
- Decorate of your choice
- Soy sauce, fish sauce, and/or hot sauce

Directions:

1. To make the filling: In a moderate-sized-sized frying pan, warm the vegetable oil on moderate heat. Put in the ground meat and sauté until it is no longer pink. Put in the green onions and cabbage and cook until tender. Put in the sugar, fish sauce, and cilantro; cook for 1 more minute. Set the filling aside, keeping it warm.
2. To make the omelets: Mix the eggs, water, and soy sauce in a moderate-sized container. Put an omelet pan on moderate heat for a minute. Put in roughly ¼ teaspoon of vegetable oil, swirling it to coat the pan uniformly. Pour roughly ¼ of the egg mixture into the pan, then allow it to rest for roughly half a minute. When the bottom is firm, flip the omelet and cook until done. Transfer to a plate and cover using foil to keep warm. Repeat to make 3 more omelets.
3. To fill the "Egg Rolls," place 1 omelet in the middle of a plate. Put ¼ of the filling slightly off-center and then roll up. Trim the ends and chop the rolls into bite-sized pieces.
4. To serve, use Bibb lettuce leaves to pick up the rolls. Immerse in additional soy sauce, fish sauce, hot sauce, or other favorite dipping sauce, and put in the decorate of your choice.

Yield: 16–20 pieces

PORK TOAST TRIANGLES

Ingredients:

- ¼ pound of big shrimp, peeled and deveined
- 1 egg
- 1 pound ground pork (the leaner the better)
- 1 tablespoon chopped cilantro
- 1 tablespoon dried shrimp
- 1 tablespoon fish sauce
- 2 cloves garlic, peeled
- 6 slices day-old bread, crusts trimmed off
- Vegetable oil for frying

Directions:

1. Fill a moderate-sized deep cooking pan with water and bring it to its boiling point. Reduce the heat, put in the shrimp, and simmer until the shrimp are opaque. Drain the shrimp and let cool completely. Coarsely cut and save for later.
2. Put the dried shrimp, cilantro, and the garlic in a food processor and pulse until a smooth paste is formed. Put in the reserved shrimp and ground pork; process once more. Put in the egg and fish sauce and process one more time.
3. Spread the mixture uniformly over each slice of bread. Chop the bread into 4 equal slices, either from corner to corner forming triangles or from top to bottom forming squares.
4. Put in roughly ½ inch of vegetable oil to a big frying pan. Bring the oil to roughly 375 degrees on moderate to high heat. Put 4 to 5 toasts in the oil, filling side down. Ensure that the toasts are not crowded in the oil or they will not brown uniformly. After the filling side is well browned, use a slotted spoon or metal strainer to flip the toasts. Watch the toasts cautiously, as the bottoms will brown swiftly. Take away the toasts to a stack of paper towels to drain. Cautiously pat the tops of the toasts using paper towels to remove any oil.
5. Serve the toasts with sweet-and-sour or plum sauce.

Yield: 24 pieces

PORK, CARROT, AND CELERY SPRING ROLLS

Ingredients:

- ¼ cup fish sauce
- ¼ teaspoon white pepper
- 1 cup bean sprouts
- 1 cup minced or ground pork
- 1 teaspoon minced garlic
- 2 cups chopped celery
- 2 cups grated carrots
- 2 egg yolks, beaten
- 2 tablespoons sugar
- 2 tablespoons vegetable oil
- 20 spring roll wrappers
- Vegetable oil for deep frying

Directions:

1. In a big frying pan, heat the 2 tablespoons of vegetable oil over moderatehigh heat. Put in the garlic and pork, and sauté until the pork is thoroughly cooked.
2. Put in the carrots, celery, fish sauce, sugar, and white pepper. Increase heat to high and cook for a minute.
3. Drain any liquid from the pan and allow the mixture to cool completely, then mix in the bean sprouts.
4. On a clean, dry work surface, put the egg roll wrapper with an end pointing toward you, making a diamond. Put roughly 2 tablespoons of the filling on the lower portion of the wrapper. Fold up the corner nearest you and roll once, then fold in the sides. Brush the rest of the point with the egg yolk and finish rolling to secure. Repeat with the rest of the wrappers and filling.
5. Heat 2 to 3 inches of oil to 350 degrees. Deep-fry the spring rolls until a golden-brown colour is achieved; remove instantly to drain using paper towels.

6. Serve with sweet-and-sour sauce.

Yield: 20 rolls

RICE PAPER ROLLS

Ingredients:

- 1 cup thin rice noodles
- 4 (8" × 10") sheets of rice paper
- 1 cup grated carrot
- 2 scallions, thinly cut
- 1 small cucumber, shredded 20 mint leaves
- 1 small bunch cilantro
- 8–10 medium to big cooked shrimp, cut in half

Directions:

1. Soak the rice noodles in super hot water until they are soft, usually ten to twenty minutes; drain. You can leave the noodles whole, or cut them into two-inch pieces if you prefer.
2. Put a sanitized kitchen towel on a work surface with a container of hot water nearby. Place a sheet of the rice paper in the hot water for roughly twenty seconds, just until soft; lay it out flat on the towel.
3. In the center of the rice paper, place 2 to 3 pieces of shrimp and ¼ of the noodles, carrots, scallions, and cucumbers. Top with mint and cilantro.
4. Swiftly roll up the rice paper, keeping it quite tight; then roll up the whole thing using plastic wrap, ensuring to keep it tight. Place in your fridge until ready to serve.
5. To serve, trim the ends off the rolls. Chop the remaining roll into pieces and remove the plastic wrap. Serve with a dipping sauce of your choice.

Yield: Servings 2–4

SALT-CURED EGGS

Ingredients:

- 1 dozen eggs
- 1½ cups salt
- 6 cups water

Directions:

1. Mix the water and the salt in a big deep cooking pan and bring to its boiling point using high heat. Turn off the heat and let cool completely.
2. Cautiously place the eggs in a container. Pour the salt water over the eggs and seal the container firmly. Put the container in your fridge and let the eggs cure for minimum 1 month.
3. To serve, hard-boil the eggs, let cool completely, then peel, slice, and enjoy.

Yield: 1 dozen eggs

SHRIMP TOAST

Ingredients:

- ¼ pound ground pork
- ¼ teaspoon salt
- ½ pound shrimp, cleaned, deveined, and crudely chopped
- 1 egg, beaten
- 1 tablespoon chopped cilantro
- 2 cloves garlic, minced
- 2 tablespoons sesame seeds
- 2 teaspoons soy sauce
- 2 teaspoons vegetable oil, divided
- 32 slices cucumber
- 8 slices of white bread, left to sit out overnight, crusts removed
- teaspoon cayenne

Directions:

1. In a small container, mix the shrimp and pork; set aside.
2. In another small container, mix the cilantro, garlic, cayenne, and salt. Pour the spice mixture over the shrimp and pork, and combine.
3. Mix in the beaten egg and soy sauce; mix thoroughly. Split the mixture into 8 parts.
4. Smoothly spread a slim layer of the mixture on each slice of bread and drizzle with sesame seeds.
5. Heat ¼ teaspoon vegetable oil in nonstick frying pan. When it is super hot, place 1 piece of bread, meat side down, in the oil. Cook until golden in color, then remove to a paper towel, blotting any surplus oil. Repeat for all of the bread sides.
6. Cut each slice of bread into four equivalent portions and top each quarter with a cucumber slice.

Yield: 32 pieces

SKEWERED THAI PORK

Ingredients:

- 1 pound pork, thinly cut into lengthy strips
- 1 tablespoon coconut milk
- 1 tablespoon fish sauce
- 1 teaspoon salt
- 2 tablespoons sugar
- 20–30 bamboo skewers, soaked in water for an hour
- 3 cloves garlic, minced

Directions:

1. In a moderate-sized-sized container, mix the sugar, salt, garlic, fish sauce, and coconut milk.
2. Toss the pork strips in the mixture to coat completely. Cover the container and marinate for minimum 30 minutes, but if possible overnight in your fridge.
3. Thread the pork strips onto the bamboo skewers.
4. Grill the skewers for approximately 3 to five minutes per side.
5. Serve with your favorite sauce or as is.

Yield: Servings 2–3

SON-IN-LAW EGGS

Ingredients:

- ¼ cup chopped cilantro
- ¼ cup vegetable oil
- 10 hard-boiled eggs, cooled and peeled
- 2 shallots, thinly cut
- 3 tablespoons fish sauce
- 1 cup light brown sugar
- 1 cup Tamarind Concentrate (Page 20)
- Dried hot chili flakes to taste

Directions:

1. Heat the vegetable oil in a frying pan on moderate heat. Put the whole eggs in the frying pan and fry until a golden-brown colour is achieved. Take away the eggs to paper towels and save for later. (If your frying pan can't hold all of the eggs easily, do this in batches.)
2. Put in the shallots to the frying pan and sauté until just starting to brown. Take away the shallots from the oil using a slotted spoon and save for later.
3. Place the brown sugar, fish sauce, and tamarind in the frying pan. Stir to blend and bring to a simmer. Cook the mixture, stirring continuously, until the sauce thickens, approximately five minutes; turn off the heat.
4. Chop the eggs in half vertically and put them face-up on a rimmed serving dish. Spread the shallots over the eggs and then sprinkle the eggs with the sauce. Decorate using cilantro and chili pepper flakes.

Yield: 20

SPICY COCONUT BUNDLES

Ingredients:

- ½ cup chopped lime segments
- ½ cup chopped peanuts
- ½ cup diced red onion
- ½ cup dried shrimp
- 1 cup shredded fresh coconut
- 1–2 jalapeños, seeded and cut
- 20–25 moderate-sized spinach leaves, washed and patted dry
- 1 cup brown sugar
- 1 cup shrimp paste

Directions:

1. Put the coconut in a moderate-sized sauté pan and cook on moderate heat until browned, approximately twenty minutes; allow to cool.
2. In a small deep cooking pan, melt the brown sugar on moderate heat, stirring continuously. Stir in the shrimp paste until well blended. Set the sauce aside.
3. Put the coconut, onion, lime pieces, peanuts, dried shrimp, and jalapeños in a moderate-sized serving container; lightly toss to blend.
4. To serve, place four to 5 spinach leaves (depending on the size of the leaves) on each serving plate. Top each leaf with roughly 1 tablespoon of the coconut mixture and sprinkle a small amount of sauce over the coconut.
5. To eat, roll up the spinach leaf around the coconut mixture and pop the whole bundle in your mouth. Pass additional sauce separately.

Yield: Servings 4

SPICY GROUND PORK IN BASIL LEAVES

Ingredients:

- ¼ tablespoon (or to taste) ground dried chili pepper
- ½ pound ground pork
- 1 shallot, thinly cut
- 1 tablespoon toasted rice powder (available in Asian specialty stores)

- 3 tablespoons fish sauce
- 5 sprigs cilantro, chopped
- Juice of 1–2 limes
- Lettuce and/or big basil leaves

Directions:

1. Squeeze the juice of half of a lime over the ground pork and let marinate for a few minutes.
2. Heat a big frying pan on high. Put in a couple of tablespoons of water and then instantly put in the pork; stir-fry until the pork is thoroughly cooked. (It is okay if the pork sticks at first — it will ultimately loosen.)
3. Pour off any fat that has collected in the pan and then put the pork in a big mixing container. Put in the remaining lime juice (to taste), fish sauce, shallot, ground chili pepper, cilantro, and toasted rice; stir until blended meticulously.
4. To serve, put the mixture in a serving container and let guests use the lettuce and basil leaves to scoop out the mixture.

Yield: Servings 4

SPICY SCALLOPS

Ingredients:

- 1 (½-inch) piece of ginger, peeled and minced
- 1 clove garlic, minced
- 1 jalapeño, seeded and minced
- 1 teaspoon vegetable oil
- 2 tablespoons soy sauce
- 2 tablespoons water
- 8 big scallops, cleaned
- teaspoon ground coriander

Directions:

1. In a pan big enough to hold all of the scallops, heat the oil on moderate heat. Put in the garlic, jalapeño, and ginger, and stir-fry for approximately one minute.
2. Put in the coriander, soy sauce, and water, stirring to blend; simmer for two to three minutes. Strain the liquid through a fine-mesh sieve. Allow the pan to cool slightly.
3. Put in the scallops to the pan and spoon the reserved liquid over the top of them. Return the pan to the stove, increasing the heat to moderate-high. Cover the pan and let the scallops steam for approximately two to three minutes, or until done to your preference. Serve instantly.

Yield: Servings 4

THAI FRIES

Ingredients:

- 1 14-ounce bag shredded sweetened coconut
- 1 cup rice flour
- 1 cup sticky rice flour
- 1 pound taro root
- 1 teaspoon black pepper
- 1 teaspoon salt
- 2 moderate-sized sweet potatoes
- 2 tablespoons sugar
- 3 tablespoons black sesame seeds
- 4 green plantains
- Water

Directions:

1. Peel the root vegetables and cut them into flat -inch-thick strips about 3 inches long and an inch wide.
2. Mix the flours in a big mixing container and mix in ½ cup of water. Continue putting in water ¼ cup at a time until a mixture resembling pancake batter is formed. Mix in rest of the ingredients.

3. Fill a moderate-sized deep cooking pan a third to a half full with vegetable oil. Heat the oil using high heat until super hot, but not smoking.

4. Put in some of the vegetables to the batter, coating them thoroughly. Using a slotted spoon or Asian strainer, put the vegetables in the hot oil. (Be careful here: The oil may spatter.) Fry the vegetables, turning them once in a while, until a golden-brown colour is achieved. Move the fried vegetables to a stack of paper towels to drain, then serve instantly.

Yield: Servings 4–8

SOUPS

ASIAN CHICKEN NOODLE SOUP

Ingredients:

- ½ cup chopped onion
- 1 carrot, peeled and julienned
- 1 cup chopped cilantro
- 1 moderate-sized sweet red pepper, seeded and julienned
- 2 cups chicken broth
- 2 star anise
- 2 tablespoons chopped ginger
- 2 tablespoons fish sauce
- 2 tablespoons vegetable oil
- 2 whole boneless, skinless chicken breasts, cut into lengthy strips
- 3 cloves garlic, minced
- 3 ounces snow peas, trimmed
- 4 ounces, cellophane noodles, soaked in boiling water for five minutes and drained
- 5 cups water, divided
- Lemon or lime wedges
- Peanuts, crudely chopped

Directions:

1. In a big deep cooking pan, heat the oil on high. Put in the onion and sauté until translucent. Put in the ginger, garlic, and cilantro, and sauté for 1 more minute. Mix in the broth and 2 cups of the water. Put in the star anise. Bring to its boiling point, reduce heat, and cover; simmer for twenty minutes to half an hour.
2. In another deep cooking pan, bring the rest of the water to its boiling point. Put in the vegetables and blanch for a minute or until soft-crisp. Drain and run very cold water over the vegetables to stop the cooking process; set aside.

3. Strain the broth into a clean soup pot and bring to its boiling point. Put in the chicken strips and reduce heat. Poach the chicken using low heat until opaque, roughly ten minutes. Put in the cellophane noodles and reserved vegetables, and carry on simmering for two more minutes. Season to taste with fish sauce.
4. To serve, ladle the soup into warm bowls. Drizzle with peanuts and decorate with lime wedge.

Yield: Servings 4 to 6

CHICKEN SOUP WITH LEMONGRASS

Ingredients:

- ¾ pound boneless, skinless chicken breast, trimmed and slice into bite-sized pieces
- 1 (14-ounce) can unsweetened coconut milk
- 1 (1-inch) piece ginger, cut into 6 pieces
- 1 clove garlic, minced
- 1 medium onion, minced
- 1 stalk lemongrass, trimmed, bruised, and slice into 2 to 3 pieces
- 1 tablespoon vegetable oil
- 2 cups wild or domestic mushrooms, cut into bite-sized pieces (if required)
- 2 tablespoons fish sauce
- 2 teaspoons prepared Red Curry Paste (Page 17) or curry powder
- 3 lime leaves (fresh or dried)
- 4 cups chicken broth
- Juice of 2 limes
- Salt and pepper to taste

Directions:

1. In a moderate-sized-sized deep cooking pan, mix the oil, onion, and garlic. Cook on moderate heat for a minute. Put in the lemongrass, curry paste, ginger, and lime leaves.
2. Cook while stirring, for about three minutes, then put in the broth. Bring to its boiling point, decrease the heat to moderate, and carry on cooking for ten more minutes.

3. Put in the coconut milk, the chicken pieces, and the mushrooms. Continue to cook for five minutes or until the chicken is done.
4. Mix in the lime juice and fish sauce. Sprinkle salt and pepper to taste.
5. Take away the lemongrass, lime leaves, and ginger pieces before you serve.

Yield: Servings 4–6

CHILLED MANGO SOUP

Ingredients:

- 1 cup plain yogurt
- 1 tablespoon dry sherry
- 1 teaspoon sugar (not necessary)
- 1½ cups chilled chicken or vegetable broth
- 2 big mangoes, peeled, pitted, and chopped
- Salt and white pepper to taste

Directions:

1. Put all of the ingredients in a blender or food processor and process until the desired smoothness is achieved. Adjust seasonings.
2. This soup may be served instantly or placed in the fridge until needed. If you do place in your fridge the soup, allow it to sit at room temperature for about ten minutes or so before you serve to take some of the chill off.

Yield: Servings 2–4

LEMONY CHICKEN SOUP

Ingredients:

- ½ cup lemon slices, including peel
- 1 cup straw mushrooms
- 1 tablespoon minced fresh ginger
- 1 whole boneless, skinless chicken breast, poached and shredded

- 1½ cups coconut milk
- 1½ teaspoons fresh hot chili pepper, seeded and chopped
- 1½ teaspoons sugar
- 2 cups chicken broth
- 2 green onions, thinly cut
- 3 tablespoons fish sauce
- 3 teaspoons lemongrass, peeled and chopped

Directions:

1. Mix the lemon slices, fish sauce, chili pepper, green onion, and sugar in a small glass container; set aside.
2. Mix the coconut milk, chicken broth, lemongrass, mushrooms, and ginger in a deep cooking pan. Bring to its boiling point, reduce heat, and simmer for twenty to twenty-five minutes. Put in the chicken and lemon mixture; heat through.
3. To serve, ladle into warmed bowls.

Yield: Servings 4–6

PUMPKIN SOUP

Ingredients:

For the broth:

- 1 clove of garlic, halved
- 1 moderate-sized leek, cut
- 1 red chili pepper, cut in half and seeded
- 1 small banana, cut
- 1 small pumpkin, peeled, seeded, and cut into little chunks
- 1 tablespoon finely chopped ginger
- 1 tablespoon Green Curry Paste
- 1½ stalks celery, cut
- 2 tablespoons butter
- 3 stalks lemongrass, peeled and thinly cut

- 3¼ cups vegetable broth
- 1 cup coconut milk
- 1 cup half-and-half
- Salt and pepper to taste

For the chicken and vegetables:

- ¾ cup cooked rice
- 1 small Japanese eggplant, cut into 4 pieces
- 1 tablespoon vegetable oil
- 1 whole boneless, skinless chicken breast, trimmed and slice into strips
- 2 kaffir lime leaves, cut into strips
- 2 red chili peppers, cut in half and seeded (not necessary)
- 2 tablespoons butter
- 2 teaspoons finely chopped ginger
- 2 teaspoons prepared Green Curry Paste
- Thai basil

Yield: Servings 4

Directions:

1. In a big pot, melt the butter on moderate heat. Put in the pumpkin, leeks, celery, bananas, chili pepper, lemongrass, garlic, and ginger; sweat for five minutes.
2. In another sauté pan, heat the vegetable oil. Put in the eggplant and sauté until just warmed through.
3. Melt the butter in a heavy-bottomed sauté pan on moderate heat. Put in the chicken strips, ginger, lime leaves, and curry paste. Sauté until the chicken is cooked, but not browned. Put in the chicken mixture to the broth.
4. Put in the half-and-half, coconut milk, and curry paste; simmer for fifteen to twenty minutes.
5. Put in the vegetable broth and heat until warm.
6. Take away the chili pepper halves. Move the broth mixture to a blender or food processor and purée until the desired smoothness is achieved. Strain if you wish, and

season to taste with salt and pepper. Pour the mixture into a clean pot and keep warm. To prepare the chicken and vegetables:

7. To prepare the broth:
8. To serve, split the rice among 4 soup bowls. Ladle the broth over the rice. Top with a piece of eggplant, a chili pepper half (if you wish), and some basil.

SPICY SEAFOOD SOUP

Ingredients:

- ¼ cup cut green onions
- 1 pound moderate-sized raw shrimp, peeled and deveined, shells reserved
- 1 quart water
- 1 tablespoon vegetable oil
- 10 (-inch-thick) slices fresh ginger
- 2 fresh serrano chilies, seeded and chopped
- 2 quarts fish or chicken stock
- 2 tablespoons fish sauce
- 2 tablespoons lime juice
- 24 fresh mussels, cleaned
- 3 stalks lemongrass, peeled and chopped
- 3 tablespoons chopped fresh cilantro
- 6–8 kaffir lime leaves
- Red pepper flakes to taste
- Salt
- Zest of 1 lime, grated

Directions:

1. Heat the vegetable oil in a big deep cooking pan. Put in the shrimp shells and sauté until they turn bright pink. Put in the stock, water, lemongrass, lime zest, lime leaves, ginger, and serrano chilies. Bring to its boiling point, reduce heat, and simmer for half an hour Strain the broth into a clean soup pot.

2. Bring the broth to its boiling point. Put in the mussels, cover, and cook until the shells open, approximately 2 minutes. Use a slotted spoon to remove the mussels, discarding any that have not opened. Take away the top shell of each mussel and discard. Set aside the mussels on the half shell.

3. Put in the shrimp to the boiling broth and cook until they are opaque, approximately 2 minutes. Decrease the heat to low.

4. Put in the mussels to the pot. Mix in the lime juice, fish sauce, cilantro, red pepper flakes, and green onions. Simmer for one to two minutes. Season to taste with salt.

5. Serve instantly.

Yield: Servings 4–6

THAI-SPICED BEEF SOUP WITH RICE NOODLES

Ingredients:

- ¼ cup fish sauce
- ¾ cup leftover beef roast, chopped or shredded
- 1 (2–inch) cinnamon stick
- 1 stalk lemongrass, tough outer leaves removed, inner core crushed and minced
- 1 tablespoon prepared chiligarlic sauce
- 1 whole star anise, crushed
- 2 (¼–inch) pieces peeled gingerroot
- 2½ tablespoons lime juice
- 3–4 teaspoons (or to taste) salt
- 8 cups beef broth
- 8 ounces rice noodles, soaked in hot water for approximately ten minutes, strained and washed in cold water
- Freshly ground black pepper to taste

Directions:

1. In a moderate-sized-sized deep cooking pan, simmer the beef broth, star anise, cinnamon stick, and ginger using low heat for thirty to forty minutes.

2. Strain the stock and return to the deep cooking pan.

3. Put in the noodles, lemongrass, shredded beef, fish sauce, chili sauce, and garlic. Bring the soup to its boiling point on moderate heat. Decrease the heat and simmer for five minutes. Mix in the lime juice, salt, and pepper.

Yield: Servings 4–6

TOM KA KAI

Ingredients:

- 1 (1-inch) piece ginger, cut thinly
- 1 (2-inch) piece of lemongrass, bruised
- 1 boneless, skinless chicken breast, cut into bite-sized pieces
- 1 teaspoon cut kaffir lime leaves
- 2 cups chicken broth
- 2 tablespoons lime juice
- 2–4 Thai chilies (to taste), slightly crushed
- 4 tablespoons fish sauce
- 5 ounces coconut milk

Directions:

1. In a moderate-sized-sized soup pot, heat the broth on medium. Put in the lime leaves, lemongrass, ginger, fish sauce, and lime juice.
2. Bring the mixture to its boiling point, put in the chicken and coconut milk, and bring to its boiling point once more.
3. Reduce the heat, put in the chilies, and cover; allow to simmer until the chicken is thoroughly cooked, approximately 3 to five minutes.
4. Take away the chilies and the lemongrass stalk using a slotted spoon before you serve.

Yield: Servings 4–6

TOM YUM

Ingredients:

- 1 can straw mushrooms, drained
- 2 stalks lemongrass, bruised and slice into 1-inch-long segments
- 2 tablespoons fish sauce
- 2 tablespoons minced fresh ginger
- 20 moderate-sized shrimp, shelled but with tails left on
- 2–3 teaspoons cut kaffir lime leaves or lime zest
- 2–3 Thai chili peppers, seeded and minced
- 3 shallots, finely chopped
- 3 tablespoons lime juice
- 4–5 cups water

Directions:

1. Pour the water into a moderate-sized soup pot. Put in the shallots, lemongrass, fish sauce, and ginger. Bring to its boiling point, reduce heat, and simmer for about three minutes.
2. Put in the shrimp and mushrooms, and cook until the shrimp turn pink. Mix in the lime zest, lime juice, and chili peppers.
3. Cover and take out of the heat. Allow the soup to steep for five to ten minutes before you serve.

Yield: Servings 4–6

VEGETARIAN LEMONGRASS SOUP

Ingredients:

- ½ cup crudely shredded carrots
- ½ cup cut celery
- 1 can straw mushrooms, drained
- 1 cup snow peas, trimmed
- 1 red serrano chili, seeded and thinly cut
- 1 teaspoon (or to taste) crushed red peppers
- 4 tablespoons soy sauce

- 4–6 stalks lemongrass, bruised
- 8 cups low-sodium vegetable broth
- Juice of ½ lime or to taste

Directions:

1. Bring the broth to a simmer in a big deep cooking pan. Put in the crushed red peppers, lemongrass, soy sauce, and lime juice. Simmer for about ten minutes.
2. Put in the rest of the ingredients. Continue to simmer until the vegetables are just done, approximately two to three minutes. Take away the lemongrass stalks before you serve.

Yield: Servings 4–6

SALADS

ASIAN NOODLE AND VEGETABLE SALAD

Ingredients:

- ¼ pound snow peas, trimmed and cut on the diagonal
- ½ cup toasted peanuts, chopped
- 1 cup bean sprouts
- 1 lime, cut into 6–8 wedges
- 1 medium carrot, peeled and thinly cut on the diagonal
- 1 recipe Spicy Thai Dressing (Page 33)
- 1 small red bell pepper, cored, seeded, and slice into fine strips
- 1 teaspoon sesame oil
- 1 teaspoon soy sauce
- 10 basil leaves, shredded (if possible Thai or lemon)
- 2 teaspoons vegetable oil
- 4 green onions, thinly cut
- 8 ounces dried rice noodles, cooked firm to the bite and washed under cold water

Directions:

1. In a big container, toss the noodles with the oils and the soy sauce.
2. Blanch the snow peas in boiling water for half a minute and then wash them under cold water.
3. Put in the snow peas, bell pepper, and the carrot to the noodles and toss.
4. Sprinkle the Spicy Thai Dressing (Page 33) over the noodle mixture to taste, put in the basil, half of the green onions, and half of the bean sprouts, and toss thoroughly.
5. To serve, put the noodle salad on a chilled serving platter. Spread the rest of the green onions, remaining bean sprouts, and the peanuts over the top. Squeeze the juice of 2 lime wedges over the whole dish, and use the rest of the wedges as decorate. Serve instantly.

Yield: Servings 4–6

CRUNCHY COCONUT-FLAVORED SALAD

Ingredients:

- 1 cup julienned jicama
- 1 medium cucumber, peeled, seeded, and julienned
- 1 recipe Coconut Marinade (Page 12)
- 2–3 tablespoons chopped fresh basil

Directions:

1. Put the jicama, cucumber, and basil in a big container.
2. Pour the marinade over the vegetables and allow to rest in your fridge for minimum 2 hours before you serve.

Yield: Servings 2–3

CUCUMBER SALAD WITH LEMONGRASS

Ingredients:

- ¼ cup minced mint
- ¼ cup minced parsley
- ½ cup shredded carrot
- ½ cup white vinegar
- 1 cup bean sprouts
- 1 cup cubed tart apple (such as Granny Smith)
- 1 garlic clove, very thoroughly minced
- 1 tablespoon fish sauce
- 1 tablespoon vegetable oil
- 1 Thai chili, very thoroughly minced
- 2 stalks lemongrass
- 3 cups thinly cut cucumber

Directions:

1. In a small deep cooking pan, mix the vinegar, chili, and garlic. Bring the mixture to its boiling point. Cover the pan, take it off the heat, and allow to cool.
2. Trim and finely cut 1 lemongrass stalk. Put it in a small deep cooking pan with ½ cup of water, cover, and bring to its boiling point. Turn off heat and allow to cool.
3. Trim the rest of the lemongrass stalk, peel off the tough outer layers, and finely mince the white portion of the soft stalk within. Reserve roughly 1 tablespoon.
4. Mix the cucumber, bean sprouts, apple, carrot, mint, and parsley in a big mixing container. In a small container mix the fish sauce, oil, minced lemongrass, the vinegar mixture, and the lemongrass water.
5. Toss the vegetables with the lemongrass vinaigrette to taste.

Yield: Servings 6–8

FIERY BEEF SALAD

Ingredients:

For the dressing:

- ¼ cup basil leaves
- ¼ cup lemon juice
- ¼ teaspoon black pepper
- 2 cloves garlic
- 2 tablespoons brown sugar
- 2 tablespoons chopped serrano chilies
- 2 tablespoons fish sauce

For the salad:

- ½ cup mint leaves
- 1 pound beef steak
- 1 small cucumber, finely cut
- 1 small red onion, finely cut
- 1 stalk lemongrass, outer leaves removed and discarded, inner stalk finely cut

- 1 tomato, finely cut
- Bibb or romaine lettuce leaves
- Salt and pepper to taste

Directions:

1. Mix all of the dressing ingredients in a blender and pulse until well blended; set aside.
2. Flavour the steak with salt and pepper. Over a hot fire, grill to moderate-rare (or to your preference). Move the steak to a platter, cover using foil, and allow to rest for five to ten minutes before carving.
3. Cut the beef across the grain into thin slices.
4. Put the beef slices, any juices from the platter, and the rest of the salad ingredients, apart from the lettuce, in a big mixing container. Put in the dressing and toss to coat.
5. To serve, place lettuce leaves on separate plates and mound the beef mixture on top of the lettuce.

Yield: Servings 2–4

GRILLED CALAMARI SALAD

Ingredients:

For the dressing:

- 1 small onion, thinly cut
- 1 stalk lemongrass, inner core finely chopped
- 1 tablespoon fish sauce
- 1–5 red chili peppers, seeded and chopped
- 3 kaffir lime leaves, chopped or 1 tablespoon lime zest
- 5 teaspoons lime juice
- 1 cup water

For the salad:

- 1 green onion, thinly cut
- 1 pound calamari, cleaned

- 6–8 sprigs cilantro, chopped
- Baby greens (not necessary)
- fifteen–20 mint leaves, chopped

Directions:

1. Mix all the dressing ingredients in a small container; set aside.
2. Prepare a grill or broiler. Put the calamari on a broiler pan or in a grill basket and cook using high heat until soft, approximately 3 minutes per side. Allow to cool to room temperature.
3. Put the grilled calamari in a mixing container. Mix the dressing and pour it over the calamari.
4. If serving instantly, put in the mint, cilantro, and green onions. If you don't like this method, allow the calamari to marinate for maximum 1 hour before you serve, and then put in the additional ingredients.
5. To serve: Use individual cups or bowls to help capture some of the wonderful dressing. If you don't like this method, mound the calamari mixture over a bed of baby greens and spoon additional dressing over the top.

Yield: Servings 2–4

PAPAYA SALAD

Ingredients:

- ½ cup long beans (green beans), cut into 1–inch pieces
- ½–1 teaspoon salt
- 1 medium papaya, peeled and julienned, or cut into little pieces
- 2 teaspoons fish sauce
- 2 tomatoes, thinly cut
- 3 jalapeño peppers, seeded and thinly cut
- 4 tablespoons Tamarind Concentrate (Page 20)
- 4–6 cloves of garlic, chopped crudely
- Sticky rice, cooked in accordance with package directions

Directions:

1. Put the papaya on a sheet pan and drizzle it with salt. Allow the papaya stand for half an hour Pour off any juice and then squeeze the fruit with your hands to extract as much fluid as you can. Put the pulp of the papaya in a big food processor.
2. Put in the chilies and pulse for a short period of time to blend. Put in the rest of the ingredients except the tomato and pulse again until combined.
3. Move the papaya mixture to a serving container and decorate with tomato slices. Serve with sticky rice.

Yield: Servings 4–6

SHRIMP AND NOODLE SALAD

Ingredients:

- ½–1 teaspoon dried red pepper flakes
- ¾ cup lime juice (roughly 4–5 limes)
- 1 clove garlic, minced
- 1 cup citrus fruit (oranges, grapefruit, tangerines, etc.) peeled, sectioned, and chopped
- 1 medium tomato, peeled, seeded, and chopped
- 1 stalk lemongrass, thoroughly minced (inner core only)
- 1 tablespoon brown sugar
- 1 tablespoon vegetable oil
- 2 tablespoons fish sauce
- 24 medium shrimp, peeled and deveined
- 3 green onions, cut
- 8 ounces rice noodles
- 1 cup chopped cilantro, plus extra for decoration
- 1 cup chopped mint leaves
- 1 cup chopped peanuts, plus extra for decoration
- Salt and ground pepper to taste

Directions:

1. Soak the rice noodles in hot water for ten to twenty minutes or until tender. While the noodles are soaking, bring a big pot of water to boil.
2. In the meantime, in a big container, combine the lemongrass, citrus, peanuts, tomato, scallions, mint, and cilantro.
3. In a small container, mix the red pepper flakes, garlic, sugar, lime juice, and fish sauce. (Adjust seasoning to your taste.)
4. Drain the noodles from their soaking liquid and put in them to the boiling water. When the water returns to its boiling point, drain them again and wash meticulously with cold water. Allow the noodles to drain well.
5. Put in the noodles and the dressing to the citrus mixture and toss to blend. Set aside.
6. Brush the shrimp with the vegetable oil and sprinkle with salt and pepper. Grill or sauté for roughly two minutes per side or until done to your preference.
7. To serve, mound the noodles in the middle of a serving platter. Put the grilled shrimp on top and decorate with peanuts and cilantro.

Yield: Servings 6

SPICY RICE SALAD

Ingredients:

For the dressing:

- ¼ cup hot chili oil
- ¼ cup lime juice
- ¼ cup sesame oil
- ½ cup fish sauce
- ½ cup rice vinegar

For the salad:

- 2 cups long-grained rice (if possible Jasmine)
- 2 carrots, peeled and diced
- 1 sweet red pepper, seeded and diced
- 1 serrano chili pepper, seeded and minced

- ¼–½ cup chopped mint
- ¼–½ cup chopped cilantro
- 1 pound cooked shrimp
- 1 cup chopped unsalted peanuts
- Lime wedges
- 4–6 green onions, trimmed and thinly cut

Directions:

1. Whisk together all of the dressing ingredients; set aside.
2. Cook the rice in accordance with the package directions. Fluff the rice, then move it to a big mixing container. Allow the rice to cool slightly.
3. Pour roughly of the dressing over the rice and fluff to coat. Continue to fluff the rice every so frequently until it is completely cooled.
4. Put in the green onions, carrots, red pepper, serrano chili pepper, mint, cilantro, and shrimp to the rice. Toss with the rest of the dressing to taste.
5. To serve, place on separate plates and decorate with peanuts and lime wedges.

Yield: Approximately 8 cups

SPICY SHRIMP SALAD

Ingredients:

For the dressing:

- 2 tablespoons prepared chili sauce
- 3 tablespoons sugar
- 4 tablespoons fish sauce
- 1 cup lime juice

For the salad:

- ¼ cup chopped mint
- ¾ pound cooked shrimp
- 1 small red onion, thinly cut

- 2 cucumbers, peeled and thinly cut
- 2 green onions, trimmed and thinly cut
- Bibb lettuce leaves

Directions:

1. In a small container, mix all the dressing ingredients. Stir until the sugar dissolves completely.
2. In a big container, mix all of the salad ingredients apart from the lettuce. Pour the dressing over and toss to coat.
3. To serve, put the lettuce leaves on separate plates. Mound a portion of the shrimp salad on top of the leaves. Serve instantly.

Yield: Servings 2–4

SWEET-AND-SOUR CUCUMBER SALAD

Ingredients:

- ½ cup rice or white vinegar
- 1 cup boiling water
- 1 small red onion, cut
- 1 teaspoon salt
- 2 medium cucumbers, seeded and cut
- 2 Thai chilies, seeded and minced
- 5 tablespoons sugar

Directions:

1. In a small container, mix the sugar, salt, and boiling water. Stir to meticulously dissolve sugar and salt. Put in the vinegar and allow the vinaigrette to cool completely.
2. Put the cucumbers, onion slices, and the chili peppers in a medium-sized container. Pour the dressing over the vegetables. Cover and let marinate in your fridge minimum until cold, if possible overnight.

Yield: Servings 2–4

THAI DINNER SALAD

Ingredients:

For the dressing:

- ¾ teaspoon rice wine vinegar
- 1 clove garlic, minced
- 1 tablespoon lemon juice
- 1 tablespoon water
- 2 tablespoons fish sauce
- 2 teaspoons sugar
- Pinch of red pepper flakes

For the salad:

- ¼ cup chopped cilantro
- ¼ cup chopped mint leaves
- 1 cucumber, peeled, seeded, and diced
- 1 small head of romaine or Bibb lettuce, torn into bitesized pieces
- 2 small carrots, grated
- Chopped unsalted peanuts (not necessary)

Directions:

1. In a small container, mix together all of the salad dressing ingredients; set aside.
2. In a big container, toss together all of the salad ingredients. Put in dressing to taste and toss until thoroughly coated. Drizzle chopped peanuts over the top of each salad, if you wish.

Yield: Servings 2–4

THAILAND BAMBOO SHOOTS

Ingredients:

- 1 20-ounce can of bamboo shoots, shredded, liquid reserved

- 1 teaspoon fish sauce
- 1 teaspoon ground dried chili pepper
- 2 green onions, cut
- 2 tablespoons finely crushed peanuts, divided
- Juice of ½ lime
- Sticky rice, cooked in accordance with package directions

Directions:

1. Put the shredded bamboo shoots and roughly ¼ cup (half) of the reserved bamboo liquid in a moderate-sized deep cooking pan. Bring the contents of the pan to its boiling point, reduce heat, and allow to simmer until soft, approximately five minutes. Turn off the heat.
2. Mix in the lime juice, chili pepper, green onions, fish sauce, and 1 tablespoon of the peanuts.
3. Serve with sticky rice, sprinkled with the rest of the peanuts.

Yield: Servings 4

THAILAND SEAFOOD SALAD

Ingredients:

- ¼ cup fish sauce
- ½ pound salad shrimp
- ½ pound squid rings, poached in salted water for half a minute
- 1 (6-ounce) can chopped clams, drained
- 1 clove garlic, minced
- 1 green onion, trimmed and thinly cut
- 1 small onion, finely chopped
- 1 small serrano chili, seeded and finely chopped
- 1 stalk celery, cleaned and thinly cut
- 1 stalk lemongrass, outer leaves removed, inner core minced
- 2 medium cucumbers, peeled, halved, seeded, and super slimly cut
- 2 tablespoons chopped mint

- Bibb lettuce leaves
- Sugar to taste

Directions:

1. In a big mixing container, gently mix the squid, shrimp, clams, cucumber, and celery; set aside.
2. In a small mixing container, mix together the onion, lemongrass, serrano chili, mint, garlic, green onion, and fish sauce. Put in sugar to taste.
3. Pour the dressing over the seafood mixture, tossing to coat. Cover and allow it to sit for minimum 30 minutes before you serve.
4. To serve, place lettuce leaves in the middle of four to 6 plates. Mound the seafood salad on top of the lettuce leaves.

Yield: Servings 4–6

ZESTY MELON SALAD

Ingredients:

- ¼ cup honey
- ¼ teaspoon salt
- 1 serrano chili, seeded and minced (for a hotter salad, leave the seeds in)
- 2 cucumbers, peeled, halved, seeded, and cut
- 6 cups assorted melon cubes
- 6–8 tablespoons lime juice
- Zest of 1 lime

Directions:

1. In a big mixing container, mix the melon and the cucumber.
2. Combine the rest of the ingredients together in a small container. Pour over the fruit and toss thoroughly to coat.
3. Serve instantly, or if you prefer a zestier flavor, let the salad sit for maximum 2 hours to allow the chili flavor to develop.

Yield: Servings 4–6

MEAT DISHES

GREEN CURRY BEEF

Ingredients:

- ¼ cup (or to taste) Green Curry Paste
- ¼ cup brown sugar
- ¼ cup fish sauce
- 1 cup basil
- 1 pound eggplant (Japanese, Thai, or a combination), cut into ¼-inch slices
- 1½ pounds sirloin, cut into fine strips
- 2 cans coconut milk, thick cream separated from the milk
- 6 serrano chilies, stemmed, seeded, and cut in half along the length

Directions:

1. Put the thick cream from the coconut milk and the curry paste in a big soup pot and stir until blended. Put on moderate to high heat and bring to its boiling point. Decrease the heat and simmer for two to three minutes.
2. Put in the beef and the coconut milk, stirring to blend. Return the mixture to a simmer.
3. Put in the sugar and the fish sauce, stirring until the sugar dissolves, approximately 2 minutes.
4. Put in the eggplant and simmer for one to two minutes.
5. Put in the serrano chilies and cook one minute more.
6. Turn off the heat and mix in the basil.

Yield: Servings 4–6

CURRIED BEEF AND POTATO STEW

Ingredients:

- ¼ cup Tamarind Concentrate (Page 20)

- ½ cup brown sugar
- ½ cup unsalted roasted peanuts, chopped
- ½–¾ cup prepared Massaman Curry Paste (Page 19)
- 1 big onion, chopped
- 1 big russet potato, peeled and slice into bite-sized cubes
- 1 cup chopped fresh pineapple
- 1½ pounds beef stew meat, cut into bite-sized cubes
- 2 (14-ounce) cans coconut milk
- 2–3 tablespoons vegetable oil
- 7 tablespoons fish sauce
- Jasmine rice, cooked in accordance with package directions

Directions:

1. Heat the oil in a big soup pot on moderate to high heat. Once the oil is hot, brown the meat on all sides. Put in the onion and cook until translucent, approximately two to three minutes.
2. Put in enough water to just cover the meat and onions. Bring to its boiling point, reduce heat, cover, and simmer for thirty to 60 minutes.
3. Put in the potatoes and carry on simmering for fifteen more minutes. (The potatoes will not be fairly thoroughly cooked now.)
4. Strain the solids from the broth, saving for later both.
5. In another soup pot, mix the coconut milk with the curry paste until well mixed. Bring the contents to a simmer on moderate to high heat and cook for two to three minutes.
6. Put in the reserved meat and potato mixture, the sugar, fish sauce, and tamarind, stirring until the sugar dissolves. Put in some of the reserved broth to thin the sauce to desired consistency.
7. Mix in the pineapple and carry on simmering until the potatoes are thoroughly cooked.
8. To serve, place some Jasmine rice in the center of individual serving plates and spoon the stew over the top. Decorate using the chopped peanuts.

Yield: Servings 4

RED BEEF CURRY

Ingredients:

- ¼ cup chopped basil
- ½ cup plus 2 tablespoons coconut milk
- 1 green or red sweet pepper, seeded and cubed
- 1 pound lean beef, cut into fine strips
- 1 tablespoon vegetable oil
- 1–3 tablespoons (to taste) fish sauce
- 2 tablespoons (roughly) ground peanuts
- 2 tablespoons Red Curry Paste (Page 17)
- Rice, cooked in accordance with package directions
- Sugar to taste

Directions:

1. Heat the oil in a big sauté pan using low heat. Put in the curry paste and cook, stirring continuously, until aromatic, approximately one minute.
2. Mix in the ½ cup of coconut milk and bring the mixture to a simmer. Put in the beef strips and poach for five minutes.
3. Put in the peanuts and continue to poach for another five minutes.
4. Put in the fish sauce and sugar to taste; carry on cooking until the mixture is almost dry, then put in the sweet pepper and basil and cook for 5 more minutes.
5. Serve with rice.

Yield: Servings 4

HOT AND SOUR BEEF

Ingredients:

- 1 green onion, trimmed and thinly cut
- 1 tablespoon dark, sweet soy sauce
- 1 tablespoon fish sauce

- 1 tablespoon lime juice
- 1 teaspoon chopped cilantro
- 1 teaspoon dried chili powder
- 1 teaspoon honey
- 1½ pound sirloin steak
- 3 tablespoons chopped onion
- Salt and pepper to taste

Directions:

1. Make the sauce by meticulously combining the first 8 ingredients; set aside.
2. Flavour the steak with salt and pepper, then grill or broil it to your preferred doneness. Take away the steak from the grill, cover using foil, and allow to rest for five to ten minutes.
3. Thinly slice the steak, cutting across the grain.
4. Position the pieces on a serving platter or on 1 or 2 dinner plates. Ladle the sauce over the top. Serve with rice and a side vegetable.

Yield: Servings 1–2

GRILLED GINGER BEEF

Ingredients:

- 1 (2-inch) piece of ginger, minced
- 1 (3-inch) piece ginger, cut in half
- 1 cinnamon stick
- 1 onion, cut in half
- 1 pound green vegetables
- 1 small package of rice noodles
- 2 dried red chili peppers
- 2 stalks lemongrass
- 2 tablespoons (or to taste) soy sauce
- 5 cloves garlic

- 6 (6-ounce) strip steaks
- 6 scallions, minced
- 8 cups low-salt beef broth
- Salt and pepper to taste

Directions:

1. Put the beef broth, lemongrass, and garlic in a big pot; bring to its boiling point.
2. Meanwhile, put the ginger and onion halves, cut-side down, in a dry frying pan using high heat and cook until black. Put in the onion and ginger to the broth mixture.
3. Put the cinnamon and dried chili peppers in the dry frying pan and toast on moderate heat for a minute; put in to the broth mixture.
4. Lower the heat and simmer the broth for a couple of hours. Cool, strain, and place in your fridge overnight.
5. Before you are ready to eat, remove the broth from the fridge and skim off any fat that may have collected. Bring the broth to a simmer and put in the minced ginger.
6. Soak the rice noodles in hot water for ten to twenty minutes or until soft; drain.
7. Blanch the vegetables for approximately one minute. Using a slotted spoon, remove them from the boiling water and shock them in cold water.
8. Flavour the broth to taste with the soy sauce. Flavour the steaks with salt and pepper and grill or broil to your preference.
9. To serve, slice the steaks into fine strips (cutting across the grain) and put them in 6 big bowls. Put in a portion of noodles and vegetables to the bowls and ladle the broth over the top.

Yield: Servings 6

THAI BEEF WITH RICE NOODLES

Ingredients:

- ¼ cup soy sauce
- ½ pound dried rice noodles
- ¾ pound sirloin, trimmed of all fat, washed and patted dry
- 1 pound greens (such as spinach or bok choy), cleaned and slice into ½-inch strips

- 2 eggs, beaten
- 2 tablespoons dark brown sugar
- 2 tablespoons fish sauce
- 2 tablespoons minced garlic
- 5 tablespoons vegetable oil, divided
- Crushed dried red pepper flakes to taste
- Freshly ground black pepper
- Rice vinegar to taste

Directions:

1. Cut the meat into two-inch-long, ½–inch-wide strips.
2. Cover the noodles with warm water for five minutes, then drain.
3. In a small container, mix the soy sauce, fish sauce, brown sugar, and black pepper; set aside.
4. Heat a wok or heavy frying pan using high heat. Put in roughly 2 tablespoons of the vegetable oil. Once the oil is hot, but not smoking, put in the garlic. After stirring for 5 seconds, put in the greens and stir-fry for roughly two minutes; set aside.
5. Put in 2 more tablespoons of oil to the wok. Put in the beef and stir-fry until browned on all sides, approximately 2 minutes; set aside.
6. Heat 1 tablespoon of oil in the wok and put in the noodles. Toss until warmed through, roughly two minutes; set aside.
7. Heat the oil remaining in the wok. Put in the eggs and cook, without stirring until they are set, approximately half a minute. Break up the eggs slightly and mix in the reserved noodles, beef, and greens, and the red pepper flakes. Mix the reserved soy mixture, then put in it to the wok. Toss to coat and heat through. Serve instantly with rice vinegar to drizzle over the top.

Yield: Servings 2–4

MINTY STIR-FRIED BEEF

Ingredients:

- ¼ cup chopped garlic

- ¼ cup chopped yellow or white onion
- ¼ cup vegetable oil
- ½ cup chopped mint leaves
- ½–¾ cup water
- 1 pound flank steak, cut across the grain into fine strips
- 1 tablespoon sugar
- 3 tablespoons fish sauce
- 7–14 (to taste) serrano chilies, seeded and crudely chopped

Directions:

1. Using a mortar and pestle or a food processor, grind together the chilies, garlic, and onion.
2. Heat the oil on moderate to high heat in a wok or big frying pan. Put in the ground chili mixture to the oil and stir-fry for one to two minutes.
3. Put in the beef and stir-fry until it just starts to brown.
4. Put in the rest of the ingredients, adjusting the amount of water depending on how thick you desire the sauce.
5. Serve with sufficient Jasmine rice.

Yield: Servings 4–6

CHILIED BEEF

Ingredients:

- ¼ cup white vinegar
- 1 big red onion, cut
- 1 pound flank steak
- 1 teaspoon dried red pepper flakes
- 2 tablespoons fish sauce
- 3 serrano chilies, stems removed and cut
- 4 scallions, trimmed and thinly cut
- Bibb or romaine lettuce leaves
- Juice of 1 big lime

Directions:

1. Put the cut chilies in a small container with the vinegar; allow it to stand for minimum fifteen minutes.
2. Grill or broil the flank steak to your desired doneness. Remove from the grill, cover using foil, and allow it to stand ten minutes. Thinly slice the streak across the grain.
3. Put the beef slices in a big container. Put in the red onion, scallions, lime juice, and red pepper flakes; toss all of the ingredients together. Cover the dish, place in your fridge, and let marinate for minimum 1 hour.
4. Before you serve, let the beef return to room temperature. Mound the beef on top of lettuce leaves and serve with white rice. Pass the serrano/vinegar sauce separately.

Yield: Servings 4–6

PORK AND EGGPLANT STIR-FRY

Ingredients:

- 3 tablespoons vegetable oil
- ½ pound ground pork
- ½ teaspoon freshly ground pepper
- 1 tablespoon fish sauce
- 1 tablespoon Yellow Bean Sauce (Page 24)
- 1 pound Japanese eggplant, cut into ¼-inch slices
- ¼ cup chicken stock
- 2 tablespoons (or to taste) sugar
- 5–10 cloves garlic, mashed

Directions:

1. Heat the oil in a wok or big frying pan on moderate to high heat. Once the oil is hot, put in the garlic and stir-fry until aromatic, approximately half a minute.
2. Put in the pork and continue to stir-fry until the pork loses its color, approximately one minute.
3. Put in the pepper, fish sauce, bean sauce, and eggplant; cook for a minute.

4. Put in the chicken stock. Continue to stir-fry for a couple of minutes.
5. Mix in the sugar to taste and cook until the eggplant is thoroughly cooked, approximately 2 more minutes.

Yield: Servings 2–4

PORK WITH GARLIC AND CRUSHED BLACK PEPPER

Ingredients:

- 4 tablespoons vegetable oil
- 1 pork tenderloin, trimmed of all fat and slice into medallions about ¼-inch thick
- ¼ cup sweet black soy sauce
- 2 tablespoons brown sugar
- 2 tablespoons fish sauce
- 2–2½ teaspoons black peppercorns, crudely ground
- 10–20 garlic cloves, mashed

Directions:

1. Put the garlic and the black pepper in a small food processor and process for a short period of time to make a crude paste; set aside.
2. Heat the oil in a wok or big frying pan on moderate to high heat. Once the oil is hot, put in the garlic-pepper paste and stir-fry until the garlic turns gold.
3. Increase the heat to high and put in the pork medallions; stir-fry for half a minute.
4. Put in the soy sauce and brown sugar, stirring until the sugar is dissolved.
5. Put in the fish sauce and carry on cooking until the pork is thoroughly cooked, approximately another one to two minutes.

Yield: Servings 2

BANGKOK-STYLE ROASTED PORK TENDERLOIN

Ingredients:

- ¼ teaspoon ground cardamom

- ¼ teaspoon ground ginger
- ¼–½ teaspoon freshly ground black pepper
- ½ cup chicken, pork, or vegetable stock, or water
- 1 teaspoon salt
- 2 (1-pound) pork tenderloins, trimmed
- Olive oil

Directions:

1. Put rack on bottom third of the oven, then preheat your oven to 500 degrees.
2. Mix the spices in a small container.
3. Rub each of the tenderloins with half of the spice mixture and a small amount of olive oil. Put the tenderloins in a roasting pan and cook for about ten minutes.
4. Turn the tenderloins over and roast for ten more minutes or until done to your preference.
5. Move the pork to a serving platter, cover using foil, and allow to rest.
6. Pour off any fat that has collected in the roasting pan. Put the pan on the stovetop using high heat and put in the stock (or water). Bring to its boiling point, scraping the bottom of the pan to loosen any cookedon bits. Sprinkle with salt and pepper to taste.
7. To serve, slice the tenderloins into thin slices. Pour a small amount of the sauce on top, passing more separately at the table.

Yield: Servings 4

CHIANG MAI BEEF

Ingredients:

- 1 pound lean ground beef
- 1 tablespoon chopped garlic
- 1 tablespoon small dried chilies
- 1 tablespoon vegetable oil
- 2 cups uncooked long-grained rice
- 2 green onions, trimmed and cut
- 3¼ cups water

- 3–4 tablespoons soy sauce
- Fish sauce

Directions:

1. In a big deep cooking pan, bring the water to its boiling point, then mix in the rice. Cover, decrease the heat to low, and cook until the water is absorbed, approximately twenty minutes.
2. Place the cooked rice in a big mixing container and let cool completely.
3. Put in the ground beef and soy sauce to the rice, mixing meticulously. (I find using my hands works best.)
4. Split the rice-beef mixture into 8 to 12 equivalent portions, depending on the size you prefer, and form them into loose balls. Cover each ball in foil, ensuring to secure them well.
5. Steam the rice balls for twenty-five to thirty minutes or until thoroughly cooked.
6. While the rice is steaming, heat the vegetable oil in a small frying pan. Put in the garlic and the dried chilies and sauté until the garlic is golden. Move the garlic and the chilies to a paper towel to drain.
7. To serve, remove the rice packets from the foil, slightly smash them, and put on serving plates. Pass the garlic-chili mixture, the green onions, and the fish sauce separately to be used as condiments at the table.

Yield: Servings 4–6

BARBECUED PORK ON RICE

Ingredients:

- 1 cucumber, thinly cut
- 1 green onion, trimmed and thinly cut
- 1 hard-boiled egg, peeled
- 1 pork tenderloin, trimmed of surplus fat
- 1 tablespoon sesame seeds, toasted
- 1 teaspoon Chinese 5-spice powder
- 1½ cups water

- 2 tablespoons flour
- 2 tablespoons rice vinegar
- 2 tablespoons soy sauce
- 2 tablespoons sugar
- Jasmine rice, cooked in accordance with package directions

Directions:

1. Cut the tenderloin into medallions roughly ¼-inch thick. Put the medallions in a mixing container.
2. Mix the sugar, soy sauce, and 5-spice powder in a small container.
3. Pour the soy mixture over pork strips and toss the strips until meticulously coated. Let marinate minimum 30 minutes, but if possible overnight.
4. Preheat your oven to 350 degrees. Put the pork pieces in a single layer on a baking sheet lined using foil. Reserve any remaining marinade.
5. Bake the pork for roughly 1 hour. The pork with be firm and rather dry, but not burned. It will also have a reddish color.
6. Put the reserved marinade in a small deep cooking pan and heat to boiling. Remove the heat and put in the peeled egg, rolling it in the sauce to color it. Take away the egg and set it aside. When sufficiently cool to handle, cut it into thin pieces.
7. Mix the flour and water, and put in it to the marinade. Bring to its boiling point to thicken, then turn off the heat.
8. Put in the vinegar and the sesame seeds. Adjust seasoning by putting in additional sugar and/or soy sauce.
9. To serve, place some Jasmine rice in the middle of each plate. Fan a few pieces of the pork around 1 side of the rice. Fan some cucumber slices and cut hard-boiled egg around the other side. Ladle some of the sauce over the pork and drizzle with the green onion slices.

Yield: Servings 2–3

LEMONGRASS PORK

Ingredients:

- ¼ cup chopped shallots
- ¼ cup coconut milk
- ¼ cup minced garlic
- ¼ cup whiskey
- ½ cup brown sugar
- ½ cup chopped lemongrass stalks (inner white portion only)
- ½ cup dark soy sauce
- ½ cup fish sauce
- 1 pound lean pork, cut into bite-sized pieces
- 1 teaspoon cayenne pepper
- 3 tablespoons sesame oil

Directions:

1. In a moderate-sized-sized deep cooking pan, mix the brown sugar, fish sauce, soy sauce, lemongrass, whiskey, shallots, and garlic. Over moderate heat, bring to its boiling point and cook until the mixture is reduced to half. Take away the marinade from the heat and let it cool to room temperature. Mix in the coconut milk, sesame oil, and cayenne pepper.
2. Put the pork and the marinade in a big Ziplock bag. Marinate the pork in your fridge for minimum three hours, or overnight.
3. Drain the meat, saving for later the marinade. Thread the meat onto metal skewers (or soaked bamboo skewers), and grill or broil to your preference.
4. Put the reserved marinade in a small deep cooking pan and bring it to its boiling point on moderate to high heat. Lower the heat and simmer the marinade for two to three minutes. Use the marinade as a dipping sauce for the pork.

Yield: Servings 2

PORK AND SPINACH CURRY

Ingredients:

- ½ cup lean pork strips

- ½ lime
- ½ pound baby spinach
- 1 cup coconut milk, divided
- 1 tablespoon <u>Red Curry Paste</u> (Page 17)
- 2 cups water
- 2 tablespoons sugar
- 3–4 kaffir lime leaves, crumbled
- 4 tablespoons fish sauce
- Rice, cooked in accordance with package directions

Directions:

1. In a moderate-sized-sized deep cooking pan, heat ½ cup of the coconut milk and the curry paste on moderate to low heat, stirring to blend meticulously. Cook for five minutes, stirring continuously, so that the sauce does not burn.
2. Put in the pork cubes, the rest of the coconut milk, and the water. Return the mixture to a simmer and allow to cook for five minutes. Squeeze the juice of the lime half into the curry. Put in the lime half.
3. Mix in the kaffir lime leaves, fish sauce, and sugar. Continue simmering for five to 10 more minutes or until the pork is thoroughly cooked. Take away the lime half.
4. Put in the baby spinach and cook for a minute.
5. Serve over rice.

Yield: Servings 1–2

THAI-STYLE BEEF WITH BROCCOLI

Ingredients:

- ½ of a 7–8-ounce package of rice sticks
- 1 cup broccoli pieces
- 1 medium shallot, chopped
- 1 pound lean beef, cut into bite-sized pieces
- 1 tablespoon preserved soy beans (not necessary)
- 1 teaspoon chili powder

- 2 cups water
- 2 tablespoons brown sugar
- 2 tablespoons fish sauce
- 2 tablespoons sweet soy sauce
- 3 tablespoons vegetable oil
- Hot sauce (not necessary)
- Lime wedges (not necessary)

Directions:

1. Heat the vegetable oil in a wok on moderate to high heat. Put in the shallot and stir-fry until it starts to become tender. Put in the chili powder and continue to stir-fry until well blended.
2. Put in the brown sugar, fish sauce, soy sauce, and soy beans; stir-fry for half a minute.
3. Put in the beef and continue to stir-fry until the beef is almost done, roughly two minutes.
4. Mix in the water and bring it to its boiling point. Put in the rice sticks, stirring until they start to cook. Lower the heat to moderate, cover, and allow to cook for half a minute. Stir and decrease the heat to moderate-low, cover, and allow to cook for about three minutes.
5. Put in the broccoli pieces, cover, and cook for a minute. Take away the wok from the heat and tweak seasoning to taste.
6. Serve with wedges of lime and hot sauce passed separately at the table.

Yield: Servings 2–4

PORK WITH TOMATOES AND STICKY RICE

Ingredients:

- ½ pound crudely chopped lean pork
- ½ teaspoon salt
- ½ teaspoon shrimp paste
- 1 tablespoon chopped garlic
- 1 tablespoon fish sauce

- 1 tablespoon vegetable oil
- 1 teaspoon brown sugar
- 2 tablespoons chopped shallot
- 20 cherry tomatoes, quartered
- 7 small dried chilies
- Sticky rice, cooked in accordance with package directions

Directions:

1. Trim the chilies of their stems and shake out the seeds. Cut them into little pieces, cover them with warm water, and allow them to soak for about twenty minutes to tenderize; drain.
2. Using a food processor or mortar and pestle, grind (or process) the chilies and salt together until a thick paste is formed. Put in the shrimp paste, shallot, and garlic. Process until well blended; set aside.
3. Heat a wok or heavy-bottomed frying pan using low heat. Put in the vegetable oil and heat for a minute. Put in the chili purée and cook for roughly three minutes or until the color of the paste deepens.
4. Raise the heat to moderate and put in the pork; stir-fry for a minute. Put in the tomatoes and carry on cooking for three to four minutes, stirring regularly.
5. Mix in the fish sauce and brown sugar; simmer for a couple of minutes. Adjust seasoning to taste.
6. Serve this beef dish with sticky rice either warm or at room temperature.

Yield: Servings 2

CINNAMON STEWED BEEF

Ingredients:

- 1 (2-inch) piece of cinnamon stick
- 1 bay leaf
- 1 celery stalk, cut
- 1 clove garlic, smashed
- 1 pound beef sirloin, trimmed of all fat and slice into 1-inch cubes

- 1½ quarts water
- 2 tablespoons sugar
- 2 tablespoons sweet soy sauce
- 2 whole star anise
- 5 sprigs cilantro
- 5 tablespoons soy sauce

Directions:

1. Put the water in a big soup pot and bring to its boiling point. Decrease the heat to low and put in the rest of the ingredients.
2. Simmer, putting in more water if required, for minimum 2 hours or until the beef is completely soft. If possible, let the stewed beef sit in your fridge overnight.
3. To serve, place noodles or rice on the bottom of 4 soup bowls. Put in pieces of beef and then ladle broth over. Drizzle with chopped cilantro or cut green onions if you prefer. Pass a vinegar-chili sauce of your choice as a dip for the beef.

Yield: Servings 4

CHICKEN DISHES

BASIL CHICKEN

Ingredients:

- 1 big onion, cut into thin slices
- 1 tablespoon water
- 1½ cups chopped basil leaves, divided
- 1½ tablespoons soy sauce
- 1½ teaspoons sugar
- 2 tablespoons fish sauce
- 2 tablespoons vegetable oil
- 2 whole boneless, skinless chicken breasts, cut into 1-inch cubes
- 3 cloves garlic, minced
- 3 Thai chilies, seeded and thinly cut

Directions:

1. In a moderate-sized-sized container, mix the fish sauce, the soy sauce, water, and sugar. Put in the chicken cubes and stir to coat. Let marinate for about ten minutes.
2. In a big frying pan or wok, heat oil on moderate to high heat. Put in the onion and stir-fry for two to three minutes. Put in the chilies and garlic and carry on cooking for another half a minute.
3. Using a slotted spoon, remove the chicken from the marinade and put in it to the frying pan (reserve the marinade.) Stir-fry until almost thoroughly cooked, approximately 3 minutes.
4. Put in the reserved marinade and cook for another half a minute. Take away the frying pan from the heat and mix in 1 cup of the basil.
5. Decorate using the rest of the basil, and serve with rice.

Yield: Servings 4

BRANDIED CHICKEN

Ingredients:

- ¼ cup vegetable oil
- 1 (1-inch) piece ginger, cut
- 1 teaspoon salt
- 1 whole roasting chicken, washed and trimmed of surplus fat
- 2 shots brandy
- 2 tablespoons black soy sauce
- 6 tablespoons soy sauce
- 8 cloves garlic, minced

Directions:

1. Fill a pot big enough to hold the whole chicken roughly full of water. Bring the water to its boiling point using high heat. Lower the heat to moderate and cautiously put in the chicken to the pot. Regulate the heat so that the water is just simmering.
2. Poach the whole chicken for twenty minutes to half an hour or until thoroughly cooked. Cautiously remove the chicken from the pot, ensuring to drain the hot water from the cavity of the bird. Position the chicken aside to cool.
3. Take away the skin from the bird and discard. Take away the meat from the chicken and cut it into 1-inch pieces; set aside. (This portion of the recipe can be done 1 or 2 days in advance.)
4. Put in the oil to a big frying pan or wok and heat on medium. Put in the soy sauces, salt, and garlic. Stir-fry until the garlic starts to tenderize, approximately half a minute to one minute.
5. Put in the chicken pieces, stirring to coat. Mix in the brandy and the ginger.
6. Cover the frying pan or wok, decrease the heat to low, and simmer five to ten more minutes.

Yield: Servings 4–6

CHICKEN WITH BLACK PEPPER AND GARLIC

Ingredients:

- 1 cup fish sauce
- 1 tablespoon whole black peppercorns
- 1 teaspoon sugar
- 2 pounds boneless, skinless chicken breasts, cut into strips
- 3 tablespoons vegetable oil
- 5 cloves garlic, cut in half

Directions:

1. Using either a mortar and pestle or a food processor, mix the black peppercorns with the garlic.
2. Put the chicken strips in a big mixing container. Put in the garlic-pepper mixture and the fish sauce, and stir until blended.
3. Cover the container, place in your fridge, and let marinate for twenty minutes to half an hour.
4. Heat the vegetable oil on moderate heat in a wok or frying pan. When it is hot, put in the chicken mixture and stir-fry until thoroughly cooked, approximately 3 to five minutes.
5. Mix in the sugar. Put in additional sugar or fish sauce to taste.

Yield: Servings 4–6

CHILI-FRIED CHICKEN

Ingredients:

- ½ teaspoon ground coriander
- ½ teaspoon white pepper
- 1½ teaspoons salt, divided
- 2 small onions, thinly cut
- 2 tablespoons vegetable oil
- 3 pounds chicken pieces, washed and patted dry
- 3 tablespoons Tamarind Concentrate (Page 20)
- 8 big red chilies, seeded and chopped

- Pinch of turmeric
- Vegetable oil for deep-frying

Directions:

1. In a small container mix the tamarind, turmeric, coriander, 1 teaspoon of the salt, and the pepper.
2. Put the chicken pieces in a big Ziplock bag. Pour the tamarind mixture over the chicken, seal the bag, and marinate minimum 2 hours or overnight in your fridge.
3. In a small sauté pan, heat 2 tablespoons of vegetable oil on moderate heat. Put in the red chilies, onions, and the rest of the salt; sauté for five minutes. Set aside to cool slightly.
4. Move the chili mixture to a food processor and pulse for a short period of time to make a coarse sauce.
5. Drain the chicken and discard the marinade. Deep-fry the chicken pieces in hot oil until the skin is golden and the bones are crunchy. Take away the cooked chicken to paper towels to drain.
6. Put the cooked chicken in a big mixing container. Pour the chili sauce over the chicken and toss until each piece is uniformly coated.

Yield: Servings 4–6

FRAGRANT ROAST CHICKEN

Ingredients:

For the marinade:

- ½ cup fish sauce
- ½ cup sweet dark soy sauce
- 1 tablespoon freshly ground black pepper
- 2 tablespoons crushed garlic
- 2 tablespoons freshly grated gingerroot

For the stuffing:

- ½ cup chopped cilantro

- ½ cup chopped mushrooms
- ½ cup cut bruised lemongrass stalks
- ½ cup fresh grated galangal
- ½ cup freshly grated ginger
- 1 roasting chicken, cleaned and patted dry

Directions:

1. Mix all of the marinade ingredients in a plastic bag big enough to hold the whole chicken. Put in the chicken, ensuring to coat the whole bird with the marinade. Put the chicken in your fridge and leave overnight.
2. Take away the chicken from the plastic bag, saving for later the marinade.
3. Put all of the stuffing ingredients in a big mixing container. Mix in the reserved marinade.
4. Fill the bird's cavity and place it breast side up in a roasting pan. Put the roasting pan in a preheated 400 degree oven and roast for 50 to 60 minutes, or until the juices run clear.

Yield: Servings 2–4

GINGER CHICKEN

Ingredients:

- 1 cup cut domestic mushrooms
- 1 tablespoon chopped garlic
- 1 whole boneless, skinless chicken breast, cut into bite-sized pieces
- 2 tablespoons dark soy sauce
- 2 tablespoons fish sauce
- 2 tablespoons oyster sauce
- 2–3 habanero or bird's eye chilis
- 3 green onions, trimmed and slice into 1-inch pieces
- 3 tablespoons chopped onion
- 3 tablespoons grated ginger
- 3 tablespoons vegetable oil
- Cilantro

- Jasmine rice, cooked in accordance with package directions
- Pinch of sugar

Directions:

1. In a small container mix the fish, soy, and oyster sauces; set aside.
2. Heat the oil in a big wok until super hot. Put in the garlic and chicken, and stir-fry just until the chicken starts to change color.
3. Put in the reserved sauce and cook until it starts to simmer while stirring continuously.
4. Put in the mushrooms, ginger, sugar, onion, and chilies; simmer until the chicken is thoroughly cooked, approximately eight minutes.
5. To serve, ladle the chicken over Jasmine rice and top with green onion and cilantro.

Yield: Servings 2

JUNGLE CHICKEN

Ingredients:

- ½ cup coconut milk
- 1 stalk lemongrass, inner portion roughly chopped
- 1 whole boneless, skinless chicken breast, cut into fine strips
- 10–fifteen basil leaves
- 2 (2-inch-long, ½-inch wide) strips of lime peel
- 2 tablespoons vegetable oil
- 2–4 serrano chilies, stems and seeds removed
- 2–4 tablespoons fish sauce

Directions:

1. Put the chilies, lemongrass, and lime peel into a food processor and pulse until ground.
2. Heat the oil on moderate to high heat in a wok or big frying pan. Put in the chili mixture and sauté for one to two minutes.
3. Mix in the coconut milk and cook for a couple of minutes.
4. Put in the chicken and cook until the chicken is thoroughly cooked, approximately five minutes.

5. Decrease the heat to low and put in the fish sauce and basil leaves to taste.
6. Serve with sufficient Jasmine rice.

Yield: Servings 2–3

LEMONGRASS CHICKEN SKEWERS

Ingredients:

- 12 big cubes chicken breast meat, a little over 1 ounce each
- 2 tablespoons vegetable oil, divided
- 2 teaspoons fish sauce
- 5 stalks lemongrass, trimmed
- Black pepper
- Juice of 1 lime
- Pinch of dried red pepper flakes
- Pinch of sugar
- Sea salt to taste

Directions:

1. Remove 2 inches from the thick end of each stalk of lemongrass; set aside. Bruise 4 of the lemongrass stalks using the back of a knife. Take away the tough outer layer of the fifth stalk, exposing the soft core; mince.
2. Skewer 3 cubes of chicken on each lemongrass stalk. Drizzle the skewers with the minced lemongrass and black pepper, and sprinkle with 1 tablespoon of oil. Cover using plastic wrap and place in your fridge for twelve to one day.
3. Chop all of the reserved lemongrass stalk ends. Put in a small deep cooking pan and cover with water. Bring to its boiling point, cover, and let reduce until roughly 2 tablespoons of liquid is left; strain. Return the liquid to the deep cooking pan and further reduce to 1 tablespoon.
4. Mix the lemongrass liquid with the red pepper flakes, lime juice, fish sauce, sugar, and remaining tablespoon of oil; set aside.
5. Prepare a grill to high heat. Grill the chicken skewers for roughly two to three minutes per side, or until done to your preference.

6. To serve, spoon a little of the lemongrass sauce over the top of each skewer and drizzle with sea salt.

Yield: Servings 4

RED CHILI CHICKEN

Ingredients:

- 1 tablespoon vegetable oil
- ½ cup coconut milk
- 1 whole boneless, skinless chicken breast, cut into bite-sized pieces
- 2 kaffir lime leaves or 2 (2-inch-long, ½–inch wide) pieces of lime zest
- 1 tablespoon basil leaves
- 2 tablespoons fish sauce
- 1 tablespoon brown sugar
- 4 ounces Thai eggplant (green peas can be substituted)
- 1–3 tablespoons Red Curry Paste (Page 17)

Directions:

1. In a big frying pan or wok, heat the oil on moderate to high heat. Mix in the curry paste and cook until aromatic, approximately one minute.
2. Lower the heat to moderate-low and put in the coconut milk. Stirring continuously, cook until a thin film of oil develops on the surface.
3. Put in all of the rest of the ingredients except the eggplant. Bring to its boiling point, reduce heat, and simmer until the chicken starts to turn opaque, approximately five minutes.
4. Put in the eggplant and carry on cooking until the chicken is done to your preference, approximately 3 minutes more.

Yield: Servings 2

SIAMESE ROAST CHICKEN

Ingredients:

- 1 clove garlic, minced
- 1 medium onion, chopped
- 1 tablespoon fish sauce
- 1 teaspoon (or to taste) dried red pepper flakes
- 1 whole roasting chicken
- 2 stalks lemongrass, thinly cut (soft inner core only)
- Salt and pepper to taste
- Vegetable oil

Directions:

1. To prepare the marinade, put the lemongrass, onion, garlic, red pepper, and fish sauce in a food processor. Process until a thick paste is formed. Place in your fridge for minimum 30 minutes, overnight if possible.
2. Spread the marinade throughout the chicken cavity and then drizzle the cavity with salt and pepper. Rub the outside of the bird with a small amount of vegetable oil (or butter if you prefer) and sprinkle with salt and pepper. Put the bird in a roasting pan, and cover it using plastic wrap. Place in your fridge for a few hours to marinate, if possible. Take away the chicken from the fridge roughly thirty minutes before roasting.
3. Preheat your oven to 500 degrees. Take away the plastic wrap and put the bird in your oven, legs first, and roast for 50 to 60 minutes or until the juices run clear.

Yield: Servings 2–4

SWEET-AND-SOUR CHICKEN

Ingredients:

- 1 (1-inch) piece of ginger, peeled and minced
- 1 green and 1 red bell pepper, seeded and slice into 1-inch pieces
- 1 pound boneless, skinless chicken breasts, cut into 1-inch cubes
- 1 small onion, thinly cut
- 1 tablespoon vegetable oil

- 1–2 tablespoons prepared chili sauce
- 2 cloves garlic, minced
- 2 tablespoons soy sauce
- 4–6 tablespoons prepared Plum Sauce (Page 34)
- 8 ounces canned pineapple pieces, drained
- Jasmine rice, cooked in accordance with package directions

Directions:

1. In a small container, mix the soy sauce, garlic, ginger, and chili sauce. Put in the chicken pieces, stirring to coat. Set aside to marinate for minimum twenty minutes.
2. Heat the oil in a wok or big frying pan on moderate heat. Put in the onion and sauté until translucent, approximately 3 minutes.
3. Put in the chicken mixture and carry on cooking for another three to five minutes.
4. Put in the bell peppers, the pineapple, and plum sauce. Cook for another five minutes or until the chicken is thoroughly cooked.
5. Serve over lots of fluffy Jasmine rice.

Yield: Servings 4

TAMARIND STIR-FRIED CHICKEN WITH MUSHROOMS

Ingredients:

- 2 tablespoons vegetable oil
- Salt and freshly ground black pepper
- 1 teaspoon sugar
- 4 ounces domestic mushrooms, cut
- ½ cup cut onions
- 1 clove garlic, minced
- 2 tablespoons Tamarind Concentrate (Page 20)
- 2 tablespoons water
- 1 cup bean sprouts
- 1 small jalapeño, seeded and minced

- ¼ cup chopped basil
- 1–2 whole boneless, skinless chicken breasts, cut into bite-sized cubes

Directions:

1. Heat the vegetable oil in a big sauté pan or wok using high heat. Flavour the chicken with the salt, pepper, and sugar.
2. Put in the chicken to the pan and stir-fry for a couple of minutes. Put in the mushrooms, onions, and garlic; carry on cooking for another two to three minutes. Put in the tamarind and water; stir.
3. Put in the rest of the ingredients. Adjust seasonings to taste before you serve.

Yield: Servings 1–2

THAI CASHEW CHICKEN

Ingredients:

- 3 tablespoons vegetable oil
- 1 big whole boneless, skinless chicken breast, cut into fine strips
- 4 green onions, trimmed and slice into 1-inch lengths
- 1 small onion, thinly cut
- ¼ cup chicken broth
- 1 tablespoon oyster sauce
- 1 tablespoon fish sauce
- 2 tablespoons sugar
- ¾ cup whole cashews
- 2–3 teaspoons Chili Tamarind Paste (page 11)
- 5–10 dried Thai chilies
- 5–10 cloves garlic, mashed

Directions:

1. In a wok or big frying pan, heat the oil on moderate to high heat until hot.

2. Put in the chilies and stir-fry for a short period of time until they darken in color. Move the chilies to a paper towel to drain; set aside.
3. Put in the garlic to the wok and stir-fry until just starting to turn golden.
4. Increase the heat to high and put in the chicken. Cook while stirring continuously, for roughly one minute.
5. Put in the green onions and onion slices and cook for half a minute.
6. Put in the Chili Tamarind Paste, broth, oyster sauce, fish sauce, and sugar. Continue to stir-fry for 30 more seconds.
7. Put in the reserved chilies and the cashews; stir-fry for 1 more minute or until the chicken is thoroughly cooked and the onions are soft.

Yield: Servings 2–4

THAI GLAZED CHICKEN

Ingredients:

- 1 tablespoon fish sauce
- 1 tablespoon minced cilantro
- 1 teaspoon chopped ginger
- 1 teaspoon salt
- 1 teaspoon white pepper
- 1 whole chicken, cut in half (ask your butcher to do this for you)
- 2 tablespoons coconut milk
- 2 tablespoons rice wine
- 2 tablespoons soy sauce
- 4 cloves garlic, chopped

Directions:

1. Wash the chicken under cold water, then pat dry. Trim off any surplus fat or skin. Put the chicken halves in big Ziplock bags.
2. Mix the rest of the ingredients together in a small container until well blended.

3. Pour the marinade into the Ziplock bags, seal closed, and turn until the chicken is uniformly coated with the marinade. Allow the chicken to marinate for thirty minutes to an hour in your fridge.
4. Preheat your oven to 350 degrees.
5. Take away the chicken from the bags and put them breast side up in a roasting pan big enough to hold them easily. (Discard the rest of the marinade.)
6. Roast the chicken for about forty-five minutes.
7. Turn on the broiler and broil for roughly ten minutes or until done.

Yield: Servings 2–4

THAI-STYLE GREEN CURRY CHICKEN

Ingredients:

- ¼ cup (or to taste) chopped cilantro leaves
- ¼ cup Green Curry Paste
- ¼ cup vegetable oil
- 2 cups coconut milk
- 3 tablespoons fish sauce
- 3 whole boneless, skinless chicken breasts, cut into bite-sized pieces
- Steamed white rice

Directions:

1. Heat 2 tablespoons of vegetable oil in a big sauté pan or wok on moderate heat. Put in the chicken and sauté until mildly browned on all sizes. Take away the chicken and save for later.
2. Put in the remaining vegetable oil to the sauté pan. Mix in the curry paste and cook for two to three minutes. Put in the coconut milk and carry on cooking for five minutes. Put in the reserved chicken and fish sauce. Decrease the heat and simmer until chicken is soft, fifteen to twenty minutes. Mix in the cilantro.
3. Serve with steamed white rice.

Yield: Servings 4–6

FISH AND SEAFOOD DISHES

BAKED REDFISH WITH LIME VINAIGRETTE

Ingredients:

- ¼ teaspoon salt
- ½ teaspoon sugar
- 1 clove garlic, minced
- 2 (6-ounce) redfish fillets, washed and patted dry (skate, sole, or flounder also work well)
- 2 tablespoons lime juice
- 2 tablespoons vegetable oil
- 2 teaspoons soy or fish sauce

Directions:

1. Put the fillets in a shallow baking dish.
2. In a small container, mix the garlic, lime juice, soy sauce, sugar, and salt, then whisk in the oil.
3. Pour the vinaigrette over the fish and bake in a 450-degree oven for six to seven minutes or until done to your preference.

Yield: Servings 2

BASIL SCALLOPS

Ingredients:

- ¼ cup shredded bamboo shoots
- ½ pound bay scallops, cleaned
- 1 (14-ounce) can straw mushrooms, drained
- 2 tablespoons vegetable oil
- 3 cloves garlic, chopped
- 3 kaffir lime leaves, julienned, or the peel of 1 small lime cut into fine strips

- 3 tablespoons oyster sauce
- fifteen–20 fresh basil leaves

Directions:

1. In a wok or frying pan, heat the oil on high. Put in the garlic and lime leaves, and stir-fry until aromatic, approximately fifteen seconds.
2. Put in the scallops, mushrooms, bamboo shoots, and oyster sauce; continue to stir-fry for roughly four to five minutes or until the scallops are done to your preference.
3. Stir in the basil leaves and serve instantly.

Yield: Servings 2–4

BROILED SALMON WITH 5-SPICE LIME BUTTER

Ingredients:

- ¼–½ teaspoon Chinese 5-spice powder
- 1 tablespoon unsalted butter
- 2 (6-ounce) salmon fillets, washed and patted dry
- 2 teaspoons lime juice
- Vegetable oil

Directions:

1. Using paper towels, wipe a thin coat of vegetable oil over a broiler pan.
2. Preheat your broiler on high, with the rack set on the upper third of the oven.
3. Melt the butter using low heat in a small deep cooking pan. Mix in the 5-spice powder and lime juice; keep warm.
4. Put the salmon on the broiler pan, skin side up. Broil for two to 4 minutes or until the skin is crunchy. Turn the salmon over and broil two minutes more or until done to your preference.
5. Move the salmon to 2 plates and spoon the butter sauce over the top.

Yield: Servings 2

CLAMS WITH HOT BASIL

Ingredients:

- 1 bunch basil (Thai variety preferred), trimmed and julienned
- 1 tablespoon vegetable oil
- 2 cloves garlic
- 2 pounds Manila clams, cleaned
- 2 small dried red chili peppers, crushed
- 2 teaspoons sugar
- 4 teaspoons fish sauce

Directions:

1. Heat the oil in a big frying pan on high. Put in the chili peppers, garlic, and clams. Mix the clams until they open, approximately 4 to five minutes. Discard any clams that stay closed.
2. Put in the fish sauce and sugar; stir until well blended.
3. Put in the basil and stir until it wilts.
4. Serve instantly either as an appetizer or with rice as a main course.

Yield: Servings 4–6

CURRIED MUSSELS

Ingredients:

- ½ cup sour cream
- ½ cup sweet white wine, such as Riesling
- 1 tablespoon lemon juice
- 1 teaspoon (or to taste) curry powder
- 2 pounds mussels, debearded and washed well
- 2 shallots, minced
- 2 tablespoons butter

Directions:

1. In a pan big enough to hold all of the mussels, melt the butter on moderate heat. Put in the shallots and sauté until tender and translucent.
2. Put in the wine and the mussels and raise the heat to high. Cover and cook, shaking the pan once in a while, until the mussels open, roughly ten minutes.
3. Take away the mussels from the pan, discarding any mussels that haven't opened. Strain the pan liquid through a strainer and return it to the pan. Bring to its boiling point, then mix in the sour cream and curry powder.
4. Lower the heat to moderate-low and put in the lemon juice. Cook for two to three minutes. Tweak the seasonings of the sauce if required with salt and curry powder.
5. Return the mussels to the broth, coating them. Reheat before you serve.

Yield: Servings 2–4

CURRIED SHRIMP WITH PEAS

Ingredients:

- 1 (10-ounce) package thawed frozen peas
- 1 (14-ounce) can unsweetened coconut milk
- 1 cup packed basil leaves, chopped
- 1 cup packed cilantro, chopped
- 1 tablespoon vegetable oil
- 1½ teaspoons Red Curry Paste (Page 17)
- 2 pounds big shrimp, peeled and deveined
- 2–3 teaspoons brown sugar
- 4 teaspoons fish sauce
- Jasmine rice, cooked in accordance with package directions

Directions:

1. In a big pot, mix the curry paste, vegetable oil, and ¼ cup of the coconut milk; cook on moderate heat for one to two minutes.
2. Mix in the rest of the coconut milk and cook for an extra five minutes.
3. Put in the fish sauce and sugar, and cook for a minute more.

4. Put in the shrimp, basil, and cilantro; decrease the heat slightly and cook for four to five minutes or until the shrimp are almost done.
5. Put in the peas and cook two minutes more.
6. Serve over Jasmine rice.

Yield: Servings 4–6

LIME-GINGER FILLETS

Ingredients:

- ½ teaspoon ground ginger
- ½ teaspoon salt
- 2 teaspoons lime zest
- 4 fish fillets, such as whitefish, perch, or pike
- 4 tablespoons unsalted butter, at room temperature
- Salt and freshly ground black pepper

Directions:

1. Preheat your broiler.
2. In a small container, meticulously mix the butter, lime zest, ginger, and ½ teaspoon salt.
3. Lightly flavor the fillets with salt and pepper and place on a baking sheet.
4. Broil for about four minutes. Brush each fillet with some of the lime-ginger butter and continue to broil for a minute or until the fish is done to your preference.

Yield: Servings 2–4

MARINATED STEAMED FISH

Ingredients:

- 1 big mushroom, thinly cut
- 1 tablespoon cut jalapeño pepper
- 1 tablespoon shrimp paste

- 1 tablespoon soy sauce
- 1 teaspoon Tabasco
- 1 whole lean flatfish (such as redfish, flounder, or bass), cleaned
- 2 green onions, finely cut
- 2 tablespoons grated ginger
- 3 tablespoons fish sauce
- Vegetable oil

Directions:

1. Swiftly wash the fish under cold water. Pat dry using paper towels. Using a sharp knife, deeply score the fish three to 4 times on each side.
2. Mix together all of the rest of the ingredients except the vegetable oil.
3. Put the fish in a big plastic bag. Pour the marinade over the fish and seal. Allow the fish to marinate for approximately 1 hour in your fridge.
4. Fill the base of a tiered steamer full of water. Bring the water to its boiling point.
5. Meanwhile, lightly coat the rack with vegetable oil. Put the fish on the rack.
6. Put the rack over the boiling water, cover, and allow to steam for fifteen to twenty minutes, until the flesh of the fish appears opaque when pierced using a knife.

Yield: Servings 4

QUICK ASIAN-GRILLED FISH

Ingredients:

- 1 tablespoon cut jalapeño chili peppers
- 1 teaspoon freshly ground black pepper
- 1 whole fish, such as sea bass or mackerel, cleaned
- 2 teaspoons brown sugar
- 3 tablespoons chopped garlic, divided
- 3 tablespoons lime juice
- 4 tablespoons chopped cilantro

Directions:

1. Swiftly wash the fish under cold water. Pat dry using paper towels. Set the fish on a big sheet of aluminium foil.
2. Put the cilantro, 2 tablespoons of the garlic, and the black pepper in a food processor and process to make a thick paste.
3. Rub the paste all over the fish, both inside and out. Firmly wrap the fish in the foil.
4. To make the sauce, place the rest of the garlic, the lime juice, jalapeño, and brown sugar in a food processor and pulse until blended.
5. Put the fish on a prepared grill and cook for five to six minutes per side or until the flesh appears opaque when pierced using the tip of a knife.
6. Serve the fish with the sauce.

Yield: Servings 4–6

ROASTED SOUTHEAST ASIAN FISH

Ingredients:

- ¼ cup chopped green onion
- 1 teaspoon salt
- 12 fresh cilantro sprigs
- 3 cloves garlic
- 4 (12-inch-square) pieces of aluminium foil
- 4 (8-ounce) fish fillets (salmon or mackerel are good choices)
- 4 small fresh red chilies, seeded, 2 left whole and 2 julienned
- 4 thin slices of gingerroot
- 8 thin lime slices, cut in half
- Zest of 1 lime

Directions:

1. Use a food processor to mix the green onions, garlic, gingerroot, the 2 seeded whole chilies, the lime zest, and salt.
2. Preheat your oven to 450 degrees.

3. Wash the fish under cold water and pat dry. Put each fillet in the middle of a piece of foil. Rub liberally with the green onion paste. Top with the cilantro leaves, lime slices, and julienned chilies. Cover the fish in the foil.
4. Put the fish on a baking sheet and roast for roughly ten minutes per inch of thickness.
5. To serve, place unopened packets on each plate. Let guests unwrap.

Yield: Servings 4

SEAFOOD STIR-FRY

Ingredients:

- ¼ cup chopped basil
- 1 can bamboo shoots, washed and drained
- 1 pound fresh shrimp, scallops, or other seafood, cleaned
- 1 stalk lemongrass, bruised
- 2 shallots, chopped
- 3 tablespoons fish sauce
- 3 tablespoons vegetable oil
- 3 teaspoons garlic, chopped
- Pinch of brown sugar
- Rice, cooked in accordance with package directions

Directions:

1. Heat the oil in a frying pan or wok using high heat. Put in the garlic, shallots, lemongrass, and basil, and sauté for one to two minutes.
2. Decrease the heat, put in the rest of the ingredients, and stir-fry until the seafood is done to your preference, roughly five minutes.
3. Serve over rice.

Yield: Servings 2–4

SEARED COCONUT SCALLOPS

Ingredients:

- ¼ teaspoon cayenne
- ½ teaspoon salt
- 1 big egg, beaten
- 10 medium sea scallops, cleaned, washed, and patted dry
- 1½ cups sweetened, flaked coconut
- 2 cups boiling water
- Salt and pepper

Directions:

1. Preheat your oven to 350 degrees.
2. Put the coconut in a small container. Pour the boiling water over the coconut, stir, and then drain through a colander. Pat dry.
3. Spread the coconut on a baking sheet and bake for about ten minutes or until golden.
4. Put the toasted coconut in a small container and mix in the cayenne and salt.
5. Flavour the scallops with salt and pepper.
6. Heat a heavy, nonstick pan using high heat until almost smoking.
7. Immerse each scallop in the beaten egg, letting most of the egg drip off, then press the scallops into the coconut mixture.
8. Put the scallops in the pan and sear for one to 1½ minutes per side until just done.

Yield: Servings 2

SNAPPER BAKED WITH FISH SAUCE AND GARLIC

Ingredients:

- ¼ cup fish sauce
- 1 tablespoon sesame oil
- 2 cloves garlic, minced
- 2 whole small red snappers, cleaned but left whole

Directions:

1. Using a sharp knife, make 3 deep diagonal slits on each side of the fish. Put the fish in an ovenproof baking dish.
2. Mix the fish sauce, sesame oil, and garlic in a small container. Ladle the mixture over the fish, ensuring it goes into the slits. Allow the fish to sit at room temperature for half an hour
3. Bake the fish in a 425-degree oven for thirty minutes or until the skin is crunchy.

Yield: Servings 2

STEAMED MUSSELS WITH LEMONGRASS

Ingredients:

- 1 serrano chili
- 2 pounds mussels, cleaned
- 2 stalks lemongrass, outer leaves removed and discarded, inner portion bruised
- 3 (½-inch) slices unpeeled ginger
- 3 cups water
- 5 cloves garlic
- Peel of 1 lime
- Tabasco to taste

Directions:

1. Put the water, lemongrass, lime, garlic, and ginger in a pot big enough to hold all of the mussels. Bring to its boiling point, reduce heat, and allow to simmer for five minutes.
2. Bring the liquid back to its boiling point and put in the mussels; cover and allow to steam for five minutes, shaking the pan every so frequently.
3. Move the mussels to a serving platter, discarding any mussels that have not opened.
4. Put in the chili pepper to the broth and simmer for another two minutes. Strain the broth, then pour over the mussels.
5. Serve the mussels with Tabasco on the side.

Yield: Servings 2–4

STEAMED RED SNAPPER

Ingredients:

- 1 recipe Thai Sauce of your choice
- 1 whole red snapper (about 2 pounds), cleaned, but left whole
- Vegetable oil

Directions:

1. Swiftly wash the fish under cold water. Pat dry using paper towels. Using a sharp knife, deeply score the fish three to 4 times on each side.
2. Fill the base of a tiered steamer full of water. Bring the water to its boiling point.
3. Meanwhile, lightly coat the steamer rack with vegetable oil. Put the fish on the rack.
4. Put the rack over the boiling water, cover, and allow to steam for ten to twelve minutes, until the flesh of the fish appears opaque when pierced using a knife.
5. Serve the sauce on the side.

Yield: Servings 4

STIR-FRIED SHRIMP AND GREEN BEANS

Ingredients:

- ½ cup cleaned shrimp
- 1 tablespoon Red Curry Paste (Page 17)
- 1 tablespoon vegetable oil
- 1½ cups green beans, trimmed and slice into 1-inch lengths
- 2 teaspoons fish sauce
- 2 teaspoons sugar

Directions:

1. Heat the vegetable oil on moderate heat. Mix in the curry paste and cook for a minute to release the fragrance.

2. Put in the shrimp and the green beans at the same time, and stir-fry until the shrimp become opaque. (The green beans will still be fairly crunchy. If you prefer your beans softer, cook an additional minute.)
3. Put in the fish sauce and the sugar; stir until blended.
4. Serve instantly with rice.

Yield: Servings 2–3

VEGETABLE DISHES

ASIAN GRILLED VEGETABLES

Ingredients:

- 1 recipe Asian Marinade
- 1 summer squash, cut into 1-inch slices
- 1 zucchini, cut into 1-inch slices
- 12 whole mushrooms, roughly 1-inch in diameter
- 12 whole pearl onions or 12 (2-inch) pieces of white onion
- 2 bell peppers (red, yellow, or green, in any combination), seeded and slice into two-inch squares

Directions:

1. Alternate the vegetables on 6 skewers (soak the skewers in water until tender if using wooden skewers).
2. Put the skewers in a pan big enough to let them lay flat. Pour the marinade over the skewers and allow it to sit for roughly 1 hour.
3. Put the skewers in a mildly oiled grill basket and place on a hot grill. Cook roughly five minutes on each side or until vegetables are done to your preference.

Yield: Servings 6

CURRIED GREEN BEANS

Ingredients:

- 1 pound green beans, trimmed Steamed rice
- 2 tablespoons Red Curry Paste (Page 17)
- 2 tablespoons vegetable oil
- 6 cups chicken or vegetable both

Directions:

1. In a big deep cooking pan, heat the vegetable oil on moderate to high heat.
2. Put in the curry paste and stir-fry for a minute.
3. Mix in the broth until well blended with the paste. Put in the green beans and bring to a low boil. Cook for fifteen to twenty minutes to reduce the liquid.
4. Lower the heat to sustain a hard simmer and carry on cooking until the beans are very well done.
5. Serve the beans over steamed rice, ladling the sauce over the top.

Yield: Servings 4–6

GINGERED GREEN BEANS

Ingredients:

- ¼ teaspoon salt
- ½ cup coconut milk
- ½ pound green beans, trimmed
- 1 stalk lemongrass, minced (inner soft portion only)
- 1 tablespoon peeled and minced ginger
- 1–3 (to taste) serrano chilies, seeded and minced
- 2 tablespoons vegetable oil

Directions:

1. In a moderate-sized-sized deep cooking pan, heat the oil on moderate to high. Mix in the lemongrass, ginger, and chilies; sauté for one to two minutes.
2. Mix in the coconut milk and the salt until well blended.
3. Put in the green beans, raise the heat to high, and cook for about three minutes or until the beans are done to your preference.

Yield: Servings 2–4

GREEN BEANS WITH MACADAMIA NUT SAUCE

Ingredients:

- ½ teaspoon cayenne pepper
- ½ teaspoon ground cumin
- ½-1 teaspoon salt to taste
- 1 bay leaf
- 1 cup coconut milk
- 1 medium onion, chopped
- 1 pound green beans, trimmed
- 1 teaspoon ground coriander
- 2 cloves garlic, chopped
- 2 tablespoons vegetable oil
- 2 tablespoons water
- 4 whole raw macadamia nuts, chopped

Directions:

1. Put the onion, macadamia nuts, garlic, vegetable oil, and water in a blender or food processor and process until the desired smoothness is achieved. Move the paste to a small container and mix in the cayenne pepper, coriander, and cumin.
2. In a moderate-sized-sized deep cooking pan, heat the macadamia nut paste, coconut milk, and bay leaf on moderate to high heat. Heat to a simmer, reduce heat, and cook until reduced to half.
3. Mix in the salt. Put in the green beans and continue simmering, stirring once in a while, until the beans are done to your preference, approximately eight to ten minutes. Put in salt to taste if required.

Yield: Servings 4–6

ROASTED ASIAN CAULIFLOWER

Ingredients:

- 1 head cauliflower, broken into florets (cut the florets in half if large)

Directions:

1. Put the cauliflower florets in a big Ziplock bag and pour marinade over them; allow to rest in your fridge for four to 6 hours.
2. Preheat your oven to 500 degrees.
3. Put the cauliflower florets in a roasting pan. Roast for roughly fifteen minutes or until soft, turning after seven to eight minutes.

Yield: Servings 6–8

GRILLED EGGPLANT WITH AN ASIAN TWIST

Ingredients:

- 4—8 Japanese eggplants (approximately 1½ pounds in all)
- Olive oil
- Salt and pepper to taste

Directions:

1. Prepare a grill or broiler. Let it achieve high heat.
2. If the eggplants are relatively large, cut in half vertically. Toss them with a little olive oil just to coat, and sprinkle with salt and pepper. Put the eggplant either in a vegetable grilling basket or directly on the grill grate or broiler pan. Cook until soft, approximately fifteen to twenty minutes, turning midway through the cooking process.
3. Turn off the heat. Drizzle with lemon juice and fish sauce.
4. Decorate using basil leaves. Serve either hot or at room temperature.

Yield: Servings 4–6

JAPANESE EGGPLANT WITH TOFU

Ingredients:

- 3 cups cut Japanese eggplant, approximately -inch thick
- ¼ pound extra-firm tofu, cut into little cubes
- 2–3 cloves garlic, finely chopped
- 4–6 tablespoons vegetable oil

Directions:

1. Heat the oil in a big frying pan on moderate to high heat. Put in the garlic and sauté until it turns golden.
2. Put in the eggplant and tofu pieces; sauté, stirring continuously, for five to six minutes or until the eggplant is done to your preference.
3. Cautiously mix in the rest of the ingredients.
4. Serve instantly to avoid discoloration of the eggplant and basil.

Yield: Servings 2–4

PUMPKIN WITH PEPPERCORNS AND GARLIC

Ingredients:

- 1 tablespoon vegetable oil
- 2 cloves garlic
- 2 cups fresh pumpkin pieces, cut into 1-inch cubes
- 30 peppercorns

Directions:

1. Using a mortar and pestle, crush together the peppercorns and the garlic.
2. Put in the vegetable oil to a big sauté pan and heat on high. Put in the peppercorn-garlic mixture and stir-fry until the garlic just starts to brown.
3. Put in the pumpkin pieces, stirring to coat.
4. Put in the water and bring the water to a simmer. After the water has been reduced to half, mix in the fish sauce and sugar.
5. Continue to cook until the pumpkin is soft but not mushy.
6. Serve as a side dish.

Yield: Servings 4–6

SOUTHEASTERN VEGETABLE STEW

Ingredients:

- ½ cup chopped cilantro
- 1 can straw mushrooms, drained
- 1 Chinese cabbage, cut into bite-sized pieces
- 1 cup cut leeks
- 1 tablespoon minced ginger
- 1 teaspoon vegetable oil
- 1 Western cabbage, quartered, cored, and slice into bitesized pieces
- 2 cups cut celery
- 2 tablespoons brown sugar
- 2 tablespoons dark soy sauce
- 3 cups bean noodles, soaked, and slice into short lengths
- 3 tablespoons chopped garlic
- 3 tablespoons fish sauce
- 4 cups roughly chopped kale
- 4 cups turnip, cut into bitesized pieces
- 5 cakes hard tofu, cut into bite-sized pieces
- 6 tablespoons soybean paste
- 8 cups vegetable stock
- Freshly ground pepper to taste

Directions:

1. Bring the stock to its boiling point and put in the fish sauce, soy sauce, brown sugar.
2. Reduce the heat, put in the vegetables and tofu, and simmer vegetables are nearly soft.
3. In a small sauté pan, heat the oil on moderate heat. Put in paste and stir-fry until aromatic. Put in the garlic and ginger, until the garlic is golden.
4. Put in the soybean paste mixture to the soup. Mix in the noodles and cilantro, and simmer 5 more minutes.
5. Flavor it with the pepper and additional fish sauce to taste.

Yield: Servings 8

SPICY STIR-FRIED CORN

Ingredients:

- 1 cup low-sodium vegetable broth
- 1 medium onion, minced
- 1 stalk lemongrass, minced (soft inner portion only)
- 1 tablespoon butter
- 2 tablespoons fish sauce Tabasco to taste
- 2 tablespoons lime juice
- 2 tablespoons vegetable oil
- 2 teaspoons lime zest
- 2 teaspoons minced garlic
- 4 cups corn kernels (fresh or frozen and thawed are best)

Directions:

1. Put the oil in a big frying pan using high heat. Put in the lemongrass. Once it starts to brown, put in the garlic, butter, and onion. Continue to cook on high, letting the ingredients brown fairly.
2. Put in the corn kernels and cook until they brown. Mix in the vegetable stock; stirring continuously, cook the mixture for a couple of minutes, scraping the bottom of the pan to loosen any burned-on bits.
3. Mix in the rest of the ingredients and cook for 30 more seconds.

Yield: Servings 6–8

STIR–FRIED BLACK MUSHROOMS AND ASPARAGUS

Ingredients:

- 1 ounce dried Chinese black mushrooms
- 1 pound asparagus spears, trimmed
- 1 tablespoon vegetable oil
- 1–2 cloves garlic, minced

- 3–4 tablespoons oyster sauce Tabasco (not necessary)

Directions:

1. Put the dried mushrooms in a container and cover with hot water. Allow to soak for fifteen minutes. Drain, discard the stems, and slice into strips; set aside.
2. Heat the oil on moderate to high in a big frying pan. Put in the garlic and sauté until golden.
3. Mix in the mushrooms and carry on cooking, stirring continuously, for a minute.
4. Mix in the oyster sauce and a few drops of Tabasco if you wish.
5. Put in the asparagus spears. Sauté for two to 4 minutes or until the asparagus is done to your preference.

Yield: Servings 4–6

THAI PICKLED VEGETABLES

Ingredients:

- ½ cup bok choy
- ½ cup cilantro leaves
- 1 big cucumber, seeded and slice into 3-inch-long, ½-inch wide strips
- 1 cup baby corn
- 1 cup broccoli florets
- 1 cup cut carrots
- 1 recipe Thai Vinegar Marinade
- 2–3 tablespoons toasted sesame seeds
- 4 cups water

Directions:

1. Bring the water to its boiling point in a big pan. Put in the vegetables blanch for two to three minutes. Strain the vegetables and shock water to stop the cooking process.
2. Put the vegetables in a big container and pour the Thai Vinegar Marinade over the top. Allow to cool to room temperature and then place in your fridge for minimum 4 hours or maximum 2 weeks (yes, weeks).

3. Mix in the cilantro and sesame seeds just before you serve.

Yield: Approximately 6 cups

THAI VEGETABLE CURRY

Ingredients:

- ¼ cup Green Curry
- ½ cup fresh minced cilantro
- 1 pound Japanese eggplant, cut into 1-inch slices
- 1 pound small boiling potatoes, quartered (or halved if large)
- 12 ounces baby carrots
- 2 cups broccoli florets
- 2 tablespoons vegetable oil
- 3 cups canned, unsweetened coconut milk
- 3 tablespoons fish sauce
- 3—4 ounces green beans, cut into 1-inch lengths

Directions:

1. In a heavy stew pot, heat the oil. Put in the curry paste two to three minutes.
2. Put in the coconut milk and fish sauce; simmer for five minutes.
3. Put in the potatoes, eggplant, and carrots, and bring to a heat and simmer for about ten minutes. Put in the broccoli and carry on simmering until the vegetables are thoroughly cooked, ten minutes.
4. Just before you serve mix in the cilantro.

Yield: Servings 4–6

THAI–STYLE BEAN SPROUTS AND SNAP PEAS

Ingredients:

- ½ pound sugar snap peas, trimmed

- 1 (1-inch) piece ginger, peeled and minced Pinch of white pepper
- 1 pound bean sprouts, washed meticulously and trimmed if required
- 1 small onion, thinly cut
- 1 tablespoon soy sauce
- 2 tablespoons vegetable oil
- Salt and sugar to taste

Directions:

1. Heat the vegetable oil on moderate to high heat in a big frying pan.
2. Put in the onion and the ginger and sauté for a minute.
3. Mix in the white pepper and the soy sauce.
4. Put in the sugar snap peas and cook, stirring continuously, for a minute.
5. Put in the bean sprouts and cook for 1 more minute while stirring continuously.
6. Put in up to ½ teaspoon of salt and a big pinch of sugar to adjust the balance of the sauce. Serve instantly.

Yield: Servings 4–6

THAI-STYLE FRIED OKRA

Ingredients:

- ½ cup tapioca flour
- ½ cup water
- 1 cup all-purpose flour
- 1 cup vegetable oil
- 1 pound small okra, trimmed
- 1 recipe chili dipping sauce of your choice
- 1 teaspoon baking powder

Directions:

1. In a moderate-sized-sized mixing container, mix the flours, the baking soda, and water to make a batter. Put in the okra pieces.

2. Heat the vegetable oil in a frying pan or wok using high heat. (It must be hot enough that a test piece of batter puffs up instantly.)
3. Put in the battered okra, a few at a time, and fry until golden.
4. Using a slotted spoon, remove the okra to paper towels to drain.
5. Serve hot with your favorite chili dipping sauce.

Yield: Approximately 20

TROPICAL VEGETABLES

Ingredients:

- ½ cup coconut milk
- 1 shallot, minced
- 1 tablespoon fish sauce
- 1 tablespoon Red Curry Paste (Page 17)
- 1 tablespoon sesame seeds
- 1 tablespoon Tamarind Concentrate (Page 20)
- 1 teaspoon vegetable oil
- 1 yellow or red bell pepper, seeded and julienned
- 2 cups bamboo shoots
- 2 cups bean sprouts
- 2 tablespoons brown sugar
- 2½ cups baby spinach leaves
- 2½ cups green beans, trimmed and slice into 1-inch lengths

Directions:

1. To make the sauce, heat the vegetable oil in a small sauté pan on moderate to high. Put in the minced shallot and fry until golden. Move the fried shallot to paper towels to drain.
2. Using a mortar and pestle, crush half of the sesame seeds and half of the fried shallots together; set aside.
3. In a small deep cooking pan, mix the Red Curry Paste (Page 17) and the coconut milk, and bring to a simmer on moderate to low heat. Put in the tamarind, brown sugar, fish sauce,

and the reserved sesame seed? shallot mixture. Decrease the heat to low and keep warm.

4. Bring a big deep cooking pan of water to its boiling point. Put in the green beans, the bell pepper pieces, and the bamboo shoots to the water and blanch for half a minute to one minute or until done to your preference. Using a slotted spoon, remove the vegetables from the water to a colander to drain.

5. Allow the water return to boiling and put in the spinach leaves and the bean sprouts. Instantly remove them from the water to drain.

6. Toss all of the vegetables together.

7. To serve, put the vegetables in the middle of a serving plate. Pour some of the sauce over the vegetables. Pass additional sauce separately.

Yield: Servings 8–10

VEGETABLES POACHED IN COCONUT MILK

Ingredients:

- ½ cup cut mushrooms
- ½ cup long beans or green beans, broken into two-inch pieces
- ½ cup peas
- ½ teaspoon cut kaffir lime leaves
- 1 cup coconut milk
- 1 cup shredded cabbage
- 1 shallot, finely chopped
- 1 tablespoon brown sugar
- 1 tablespoon green peppercorns, tied together in a small pouch made from a Handi Wipe
- 1 tablespoon soy sauce
- 1 tablespoon Thai chilies, seeded and finely cut
- Rice, cooked in accordance with package directions

Directions:

1. In a deep cooking pan bring the coconut milk to a gentle simmer moderate heat. Mix in the shallots, soy sauce, brown sugar, green peppercorn pouch, and lime leaves. Simmer for 1 until aromatic.
2. Put in the green beans, mushrooms, and cabbage, and return simmer. Cook for five to ten minutes or until soft.
3. Put in the peas and cook 1 more minute. Take away the pouch before you serve over rice.

Yield: Servings 2–4

VEGETARIAN STIR-FRY

Ingredients:

- ¼ cup asparagus tips
- ¼ cup bean sprouts
- ¼ cup bite-sized pieces bell pepper
- ¼ cup broccoli florets
- ¼ cup cauliflower florets
- ¼ cup cut mushrooms
- ¼ cup snow peas
- ¼ cup thinly cut celery
- ¼ cup water chestnuts
- 1 small onion, cut
- 1 tablespoon cornstarch, dissolved in a little water
- 1-2 tablespoons vegetable oil
- 2 cups bite-sized tofu pieces
- 2 tablespoons dark sweet soy sauce
- 2 tablespoons grated ginger
- 2 tablespoons minced garlic
- 4 tablespoons seeded and cut Thai chilies
- 4 tablespoons soy sauce
- Rice, cooked in accordance with package directions

Directions:

1. Heat 1 tablespoon of oil in a big frying pan or wok over moderate-heat. Put in the tofu and sauté until a golden-brown colour is achieved. Move paper towels to drain.
2. Put in additional oil to the frying pan if required, and stir-fry the ginger, and chilies to release their fragrance, approximately 2 to Mix in the soy sauces and raise the heat to high.
3. Put in the reserved tofu and all the vegetables apart from the bean stir-fry for a minute.
4. Put in the cornstarch mixture and stir-fry for one more minute or until the vegetables are just thoroughly cooked and the sauce has thickened somewhat.
5. Put in the bean sprouts, stirring for a short period of time to warm them.
6. Serve over rice.

Yield: Servings 4–6 as a main course

NOODLE DISHES

BROCCOLI NOODLES WITH GARLIC AND SOY

Ingredients:

- 1 pound broccoli, trimmed into bite-sized florets
- 1 tablespoon sugar
- 1 tablespoon sweet soy sauce
- 1–2 tablespoons vegetable oil
- 16 ounces rice noodles
- 2 cloves garlic, minced
- 2 tablespoons soy sauce
- Fish sauce
- Hot sauce
- Lime wedges

Directions:

1. Bring a pot of water to boil using high heat. Drop in the broccoli and blanch until soft-crisp or to your preference. Drain and save for later.
2. Soak the rice noodles in hot water until soft, approximately ten minutes.
3. In a big sauté pan, heat the vegetable oil on medium. Put in the garlic and stir-fry until golden. Put in the soy sauces and the sugar, stirring until the sugar has thoroughly blended.
4. Put in the reserved noodles, tossing until thoroughly coated with the sauce. Put in the broccoli and toss to coat.
5. Serve instantly with hot sauce, fish sauce, and lime wedges on the side.

Yield: Servings 2–4

CHIANG MAI CURRIED NOODLES

Ingredients:

- ¼ pound ground pork
- ½ cup coconut milk
- 1 tablespoon chopped garlic
- 1 tablespoon curry powder Pinch of turmeric powder
- 1 tablespoon Red Curry Paste (Page 17)
- 1 teaspoon lime juice
- 2 tablespoons fish sauce Pinch of sugar
- 4 ounces rice noodles, soaked in water for twenty minutes to half an hour or until tender Lime wedges, for decoration

Directions:

1. Heat the coconut milk in a wok or heavy frying pan on moderate heat. Mix in the curry paste and cook until aromatic and a thin film of oil separates out.
2. Put in the garlic and cook for approximately half a minute. Put in the remainingingredients apart from the pork, noodles, and limes, and cook until the sauce thickens slightly, stirring continuously.
3. Put in the pork and continue to stir until the meat is thoroughly cooked. Decrease the heat and keep the sauce warm.
4. Bring a pan of water to a rolling boil. Put the noodles in a wire basket or strainer and immerse the noodles in the water for ten to twenty seconds. Drain the noodles and move to serving plate.
5. Pour the sauce over the noodles. Serve with lime wedges.

Yield: Servings 1–2

CLEAR NOODLES WITH BAKED SHRIMP

Ingredients:

- ¼ cup chopped cilantro
- 1 7-ounce package rice noodles
- 1 medium onion, thinly cut

- 1 tablespoon soy or fish sauce Sesame oil to taste
- 1 tablespoon vegetable oil
- 1 teaspoon sugar
- 2 cloves garlic, chopped
- 20–30 black peppercorns
- 6 big shrimp, shell on, washed and patted dry

Directions:

1. Soak the noodles in hot water until soft, approximately ten minutes. Drain and save for later.
2. Using a mortar and pestle or a food processor, meticulously mix the garlic, cilantro, and peppercorns.
3. Put in the vegetable oil to a wok or big frying pan using low heat. Put in the garlic mixture and stir-fry for a minute. Put in the cut onion and carry on cooking until the onion is soft, then remove the heat.
4. Put in the sugar, soy sauce, and a few drops of sesame oil to the wok; stir until blended. Put in the noodles and toss to coat. Pour the noodle mixture into an ovenproof baking dish. Put the whole shrimp on top of the noodles, cover the dish, and bake for about twenty minutes in a 400-degree oven. Serve instantly.

Yield: Servings 2

CURRIED RICE NOODLES WITH TOFU AND EGG

Ingredients:

- ½ of a 7-ounce package rice noodles
- ½ teaspoon ground coriander
- ½ teaspoon ground cumin
- 1 cup bean sprouts
- 1 cup coconut milk
- 1 cup cubed extra-firm tofu
- 1 green onion, trimmed and thinly cut
- 1 hard-boiled egg, cut

- 1 tablespoon <u>Red Curry Paste</u> (Page 17)
- 1 teaspoon curry powder
- 2 tablespoons chopped cilantro
- 2 tablespoons fish sauce
- 2 tablespoons minced shallots
- 2 tablespoons sugar
- 2–3 cups water

Directions:

1. In a small container, meticulously mix the coriander, cumin, curry powder, and curry paste.
2. Pour the coconut milk into a moderate-sized deep cooking pan. Mix in the curry paste mixture and place on moderate heat. Heat to a simmer and cook for approximately five minutes or until a slim layer of yellow oil starts to make on the surface of the sauce.
3. Mix in 2 cups of the water, the shallots, sugar, and fish sauce. Return the sauce to a simmer and allow to cook thirty minutes, stirring once in a while and putting in extra water if required.
4. In the meantime, soak the noodles in hot water for about ten minutes or until tender.
5. To serve, mound the noodles into serving bowls. Top the noodles with the cut egg, tofu, and bean sprouts. Ladle some of the curry sauce over top. Drizzle with green onion slices and chopped cilantro.

Yield: Servings 2 as a main course or 4 as an appetizer.

FIRE NOODLES

Ingredients:

- fifteen–20 (or to taste) Thai bird chilies, stemmed and seeded
- 1 pound presliced fresh rice noodles (available at Asian grocery stores and on the Internet)
- 2 tablespoons vegetable oil
- 2 whole boneless, skinless chicken breasts, cut into bite-sized pieces
- 2 tablespoons fish sauce

- 2 tablespoons sweet black soy sauce
- 1 tablespoon oyster sauce
- 1 teaspoon white pepper
- 1½ tablespoons sugar
- 1 (8-ounce) can bamboo shoots, drained
- 1½ cups loose-packed basil and/or mint
- 5–10 (or to taste) cloves garlic

Directions:

1. Put the chilies and garlic cloves in a food processor and pulse until meticulously mashed together; set aside.
2. Bring a kettle of water to its boiling point. Put the noodles in a big colander and pour the hot water over them. Cautiously unfold and separate the noodles; set aside.
3. Heat the oil in a wok or big frying pan on moderate to high heat. When it is fairly hot, cautiously put in the reserved chili-garlic mixture and stir-fry for fifteen seconds to release the aromas.
4. Increase the heat to high, put in the chicken, and stir-fry until it starts to lose its color, approximately half a minute.
5. Mix in the fish sauce, soy sauce, oyster sauce, white pepper, and sugar.
6. Put in the noodles and continue to stir-fry for half a minute, tossing them with the other ingredients.
7. Put in the bamboo shoots and cook for one more minute.
8. Remove the heat and put in the basil.

Yield: Servings 4–6

FLOWERED LIME NOODLES

Ingredients:

- 1 tablespoon salted butter
- 2–3 tablespoons lime juice
- 4 ounces grated Parmesan cheese
- 8 ounces angel hair pasta

- Black pepper
- Lime slices
- Rose petals or other organic edible flowers

Directions:

1. Bring a big pot of water to its boiling point using high heat. Put in pasta and cook in accordance with package instructions; drain.
2. Toss the pasta with butter, lime juice, and parmesan.
3. To serve, top with rose or flower petals and lime slices. Pass black pepper at the table.

Yield: Servings 4

PAD THAI

Ingredients:

- ¼ cup brown sugar
- ¼ cup chopped chives
- ¼ cup fish sauce
- ½ cup chopped roasted peanuts
- ½ cup cooked salad shrimp
- 1 cup bean sprouts
- 1 medium egg, beaten
- 2 tablespoons chopped shallots
- 2 tablespoons vegetable oil
- 5–6 cloves garlic, finely chopped
- 6–8 teaspoons Tamarind Concentrate (Page 20)
- 8 ounces rice noodles

Garnish:

- ½ cup bean sprouts
- ½ cup chopped chives
- ½ cup crudely ground roasted peanuts

- 1 lime cut into wedges
- 1 tablespoon fish sauce
- 1 tablespoon lime juice
- 1 tablespoon Tamarind Concentrate (**Page** 20)

Directions:

1. Soak the noodles in water at room temperature for thirty minutes or until tender. Drain and save for later.
2. Heat the vegetable oil in a wok or frying pan on moderate to high heat. Put in the garlic and shallots, and for a short period of time stir-fry until they start to change color.
3. Put in the reserved noodles and all the rest of the ingredients except the egg and the bean sprouts, and stir-fry until hot.
4. While continuously stirring, slowly sprinkle in the beaten egg.
5. Put in the bean sprouts and cook for no more than another half a minute.
6. In a small container combine all of the decorate ingredients apart from the lime wedges.
7. To serve, position the Pad Thai on a serving platter. Top with the decorate and surround with lime wedges.

Yield: Servings 2–4

PANANG MUSSELS AND NOODLES

Ingredients:

- ¼ cup white wine
- 1 medium onion, chopped
- 1 pound Asian egg noodles
- 1 pound mussels, washed and debearded
- 1 teaspoon Black Bean Paste (**Page** 10)
- 2 cups chicken broth
- 2 tablespoons vegetable oil
- 6—8 stalks celery, chopped

Directions:

1. Bring a big pot of water to its boiling point using high heat. Put in the noodles and cook until firm to the bite. Wash the noodles under cold water and save for later.
2. Heat the oil in a big sauté pan on moderate heat. Put in the Black Bean Paste, onion, and celery, and sauté for five minutes.
3. Put in the wine and chicken broth, and bring to its boiling point.
4. Put in the mussels and decrease the heat to low; cover and steam for five minutes.
5. To serve, split the noodles between 4 soup plates. Split the mussels between the plates (discarding any that have not opened) and pour the broth over the top.

Yield: Servings 4

PAN–FRIED NOODLES

Ingredients:

- ¼ cup minced chives
- ¾ pound fresh lo mein noodles or angel hair pasta
- 2 tablespoons (or to taste) prepared chili-garlic paste
- 3 tablespoons vegetable oil, divided
- Salt to taste

Directions:

1. Boil the noodles in a big pot for no more than two to three minutes. Drain, wash under cold water, and drain once more.
2. Put in the chives, chili paste, 1 tablespoon of the oil, and salt to the noodles; toss to coat, and tweak seasonings.
3. In a heavy-bottomed 10-inch frying pan, heat the rest of the oil on moderate to high heat. When it is hot, put in the noodle mixture, spreading uniformly. Push the noodles into the pan using the back of a spatula. Cook for roughly two minutes. Decrease the heat and carry on cooking until the noodles are well browned. Flip the noodles over in 1 piece. Carry on cooking until browned, putting in additional oil if required.
4. To serve, chop the noodles into wedges.

Yield: Servings 6–8

POACHED CHICKEN BREAST WITH PEANUT SAUCE AND NOODLES

Ingredients:

- ¼ cup chicken stock
- ¼ cup lime juice
- ¼cup half-and-half
- 1 cup crispy peanut butter
- 1 pound Chinese egg noodles (mein)
- 1 pound snow peas, trimmed and blanched
- 1 tablespoon peanut oil
- 1 tablespoon sesame oil
- 1½ cups coconut milk
- 2 tablespoons fish sauce
- 2 teaspoons brown sugar
- 3 whole boneless, skinless chicken breasts, halved and poached
- 4 cloves garlic, minced
- 6–8 green onions, trimmed and thinly cut
- Salt and pepper to taste

Directions:

1. Mix the peanut butter, coconut milk, fish sauce, lime juice, brown sugar, garlic, salt, and pepper in a small deep cooking pan using low heat. Cook until the desired smoothness is achieved and thick, stirring regularly.
2. Move to a blender and purée.
3. Put in the chicken stock and half-and-half, and blend; set aside.
4. Bring a big pot of water to its boiling point. Put in the noodles and cook until firm to the bite. Drain, wash under cold water, and drain once more.
5. Toss the noodles with the peanut and sesame oils.
6. To serve, place some pasta in the center of each serving plate. Ladle some of the peanut sauce over the pasta. Slice each chicken breast on the diagonal. Move 1 cut breast to the

top of each portion of noodles. Ladle some additional peanut sauce over the chicken. Surround the noodles with the snow peas. Decorate using the cut green onions.

Yield: Servings 6

RICE STICK NOODLES WITH CHICKEN AND VEGETABLES

Ingredients:

Noodles:

- 1 tablespoon sweet black soy sauce
- 2 tablespoons vegetable oil
- 8 ounces rice stick noodles

Chicken and vegetables:

- ¼ cup chicken broth
- ¼– cup cut green onions
- ¼ pound broccoli, chopped
- ½ teaspoon Tabasco
- 1 big whole boneless, skinless chicken breast, cut into bite-sized strips
- 1 cup bean sprouts
- 1 small onion, finely cut
- 1 small red bell pepper, seeded and slice into strips
- 1 tablespoon cornstarch mixed with
- 1 tablespoon water
- 1¼ cups cut Japanese eggplant
- 2 tablespoons fish sauce
- 2 tablespoons vegetable oil
- 2 tablespoons Yellow Bean Sauce (Page 24)
- 3 tablespoons brown sugar
- 4 cloves garlic, chopped

Yield: Servings 2–4

NOODLES:

1. Soak the noodles in warm water for fifteen minutes or until soft; drain.
2. Put a wok on moderate to high heat and put in the vegetable oil. Once the oil is hot, put in the noodles and stir-fry vigorously until they are thoroughly heated, approximately 45 seconds to one minute.
3. Put in the soy sauce and continue to stir-fry for 1 more minute.
4. Put the noodles on a serving platter, covered in foil, in a warm oven until ready to serve.

CHICKEN AND VEGETABLES:

1. Put a wok on moderate to high heat and put in the vegetable oil. Once the oil is hot, put in the garlic and stir-fry for a short period of time to release its aroma.
2. Put in the chicken and cook until it begins to become opaque.
3. Put in the broccoli and stir-fry for half a minute.
4. Put in the onion and eggplant and stir-fry for a couple of minutes.
5. Put in the Tabasco, fish sauce, yellow bean sauce, and sugar. Stir-fry for a minute.
6. Put in the broth, cornstarch mixture, bean sprouts, green onions, and red bell pepper; cook until vegetables are soft-crisp.
7. To serve, ladle the chicken and vegetable mixture over the reserved noodles.

SESAME NOODLES WITH VEGGIES

Ingredients:

- 1 red bell pepper, seeded and slice into strips
- 1 tablespoon sesame oil
- 2 cloves garlic, minced
- 2 cups broccoli, cut into bite-sized pieces
- 2 tablespoons vegetable oil
- 2 tablespoons water
- 2–3 tablespoons prepared chili sauce
- 2–3 tablespoons soy sauce
- 3 tablespoons sesame seeds

- 4 ounces tofu, cut into bitesized cubes
- 8 ounces egg noodles

Directions:

1. Heat the oil in a big Sauté pan or wok on moderate heat. Put in the garlic and sauté until golden, roughly two minutes.
2. Put in the broccoli and red bell pepper, and stir-fry for two to three minutes. Put in the water, cover, and let the vegetables steam until soft, roughly five minutes.
3. Bring a big pot of water to boil. Put in the noodles and cook until firm to the bite; drain.
4. While the noodles are cooking, put in the rest of the ingredients to the broccoli mixture. Turn off the heat, put in the noodles, and toss to blend.

Yield: Servings 2–4

SPICY EGG NOODLES WITH SLICED PORK

Ingredients:

- ½ teaspoon vegetable oil
- 1 cup bean sprouts
- 1 package fresh angel hair pasta
- 1 small Barbecued Pork
- 1 small cabbage, shredded
- 2 scallions, trimmed and thinly cut
- 2 tablespoons fish sauce
- 2 tablespoons sugar
- 2 teaspoons chopped cilantro
- 2 teaspoons ground dried red chili pepper (or to taste)
- 4 tablespoons minced garlic
- 4–6 tablespoons rice vinegar
- Freshly ground black pepper to taste
- Tenderloin, thinly cut

Directions:

1. Bring a big pot of water to its boiling point using high heat. Put in the cabbage and blanch about half a minute. Using a slotted spoon, remove the cabbage from the boiling water; set aside.
2. Allow the water return to boiling. Put in the bean sprouts and blanch for ten seconds. Using a slotted spoon, remove the sprouts from the water; set aside.
3. Return the water to boiling. Put in the fresh angel hair pasta and cook in accordance with package directions. Drain the pasta and place it in a big mixing container.
4. In a small sauté pan, heat the vegetable oil on moderate heat. Put in the garlic and sauté until golden. Turn off the heat. Mix in the fish sauce, sugar, rice vinegar, and dried chili pepper.
5. Pour the sauce over the pasta and toss to coat.
6. To serve, split the cabbage and the bean sprouts into 2 to 4 portions and place in the middle of serving plates. Split the noodles into 2 to 4 portions and place over the cabbage and sprouts. Split the pork slices over the noodles. Grind black pepper to taste over the noodles and top with the cut scallions and chopped cilantro.

Yield: Servings 2 as a main course or 4 as an appetizer.

THAI NOODLES WITH CHICKEN AND PORK

Ingredients:

For the sauce:

- ¼ teaspoon white pepper
- ½ cup peanut butter
- ½ cup soy sauce
- 1 teaspoon hot chili oil
- 1 teaspoon minced garlic
- 3 tablespoons honey
- 3 tablespoons sesame oil

For the noodles:

- ½ pound boneless pork tenderloin, cut into fine strips

- ½ pound boneless, skinless chicken breast, cut thin
- ½ teaspoon minced garlic
- 1 big yellow onion, diced
- 1 pound dry flat Asian noodles
- 1 tablespoon vegetable oil
- 1 teaspoon sesame oil
- 6 ounces salad shrimp
- 6–8 green onions, trimmed, white portions cut, green portions julienned

Directions:

1. Put all of the sauce ingredients in a blender and pulse until smooth; set aside.
2. Bring a big pot of water to boil using high heat. Prepare the noodles in accordance with package directions, drain, and mix in the sauce mixture, saving for later ¼ cup; set aside.
3. Heat the oils in a big sautée pan using high heat. Put in the garlic and sautée for a short period of time.
4. Put in the chicken, pork, and onion, and sauté for five to six minutes or until the meats are thoroughly cooked.
5. Put in the white portion of the green onion and the shrimp and sautée for two more minutes.
6. Put in the green parts of the onions and the rest of the sauce, stirring until everything is thoroughly coated.
7. To serve, put the noodles on a big platter and top with the meat sautée. Pass additional hot chili oil separately.

Yield: Servings 4–6

RICE DISHES

BASIC STICKY RICE

Ingredients:

- 1 cup glutinous rice
- Water

Directions:

1. Put the rice in a container, completely cover it with water, and allow to soak overnight. Drain before you use.
2. Coat a steamer basket or colander with moistened cheesecloth. (This prevents the grains of rice from falling through the holes in the colander.)
3. Spread the rice over the cheesecloth as uniformly as you can.
4. Bring a pan of water with a cover to a rolling boil. Put the basket over the boiling water, ensuring that the bottom of it doesn't come in contact with the water. Cover firmly and allow to steam for about twenty-five minutes.

Yield: Servings 2–4

BASIC WHITE RICE

Ingredients:

- 1 cup long-grain rice (such as Jasmine)
- 2 cups water

Directions:

1. Put the rice in a colander and run under cool water.
2. Put the rice and the water in a moderate-sized pot. Stir for a short period of time. Bring to a rolling boil on moderate to high heat. Decrease the heat to low, cover, and simmer for eighteen to twenty minutes.

3. Take away the rice from the heat, keeping it covered, and allow it to rest for minimum ten minutes.
4. Fluff the rice just before you serve.

Yield: Servings 2–4

CHICKEN FRIED RICE

Ingredients:

- ¼ cup chicken stock
- ¼ cup dry sherry
- ¼ cup fish sauce
- ½ medium head Chinese cabbage, crudely chopped
- 1 cup shredded, cooked chicken
- 1 cup snow peas, trimmed and slice into bite-sized pieces
- 1 medium onion, cut
- 1 tablespoon minced garlic
- 1 tablespoon minced ginger
- 1 tablespoon vegetable oil
- 2 eggs, beaten
- 3 cups cooked long-grain white rice

Directions:

1. In a big frying pan or wok, heat the oil on moderate to low heat. Put in the garlic, ginger, and onion, and stir-fry for five minutes or until the onion becomes translucent.
2. Put in the cabbage, raise the heat to moderate, and stir-fry for about ten minutes.
3. Put in the rice and stir-fry for a couple of minutes.
4. Mix the fish sauce, sherry, and stock in a small container; put in to the wok and stir until blended.
5. Put in the snow peas and chicken; stir-fry for a couple of minutes more.
6. Move the rice to the sides of the wok, making a hole in the center. Pour the eggs into the hole and cook for approximately 1 minute, stirring the eggs using a fork. Fold the cooked eggs into the fried rice.

Yield: Servings 4–6

CURRIED RICE

Ingredients:

- ¼ cup golden raisins (regular raisins can be substituted)
- ½ cup finely chopped onion
- 1 teaspoon curry powder
- 1½ cups long-grained rice
- 2 tablespoons vegetable oil
- 2 teaspoons Mango Chutney (Page 221)
- 2¾ cups vegetable stock
- Salt to taste

Directions:

1. In a moderate-sized-sized pot, heat the oil on moderate heat. Put in the onions and sautée. for a couple of minutes, until the onions are tender but not browned.
2. Put in the rice and continue to sautée. for another two minutes. Put in the curry powder and sauté for 1 more minute.
3. Pour in the vegetable stock and sprinkle with salt. Bring to its boiling point, then decrease the heat and cover. Simmer the rice for fifteen to twenty minutes, stirring once in a while.
4. Put in the raisins and the chutney. Continue to simmer for another five minutes or until soft.

Yield: Servings 4–6

DILL RICE

Ingredients:

- 1 cup long-grained rice (such as Jasmine)
- 1 green chili pepper, seeded and minced

- 1½ cups water
- 2 green cardamom pods
- 2 tablespoons vegetable oil
- 4 tablespoons chopped fresh dill
- Salt

Directions:

1. In a moderate-sized-sized pot, heat the vegetable oil on moderate heat. Put in the cardamom pods and sauté for a minute. Put in the chili and sautée. for a short period of time. Mix in the salt and the dill and cook for another two to three minutes. Put in the rice and sauté for 3 more minutes.
2. Mix in the water and bring the mixture to its boiling point. Decrease the heat, cover, and simmer for twenty to twenty-five minutes or until the liquid has been absorbed.
3. Take away the cardamom pods and fluff the rice before you serve.

Yield: Servings 2–4

FAR EAST FRIED RICE

Ingredients:

- ¼ cup chopped mint or cilantro leaves
- ¼ cup roasted peanuts, chopped
- 1 bunch green onions, trimmed and thinly cut
- 1 teaspoon dried red chili pepper flakes
- 1½ tablespoons rice vinegar
- 2 big carrots, peeled and crudely shredded
- 2 cups bean sprouts, trimmed if required
- 2 eggs, beaten
- 2 tablespoons fish sauce
- 2 tablespoons minced garlic
- 2 tablespoons sugar
- 2½ tablespoons vegetable oil

- 5 cups day-old long-grain white rice, clumps broken up

Directions:

1. Mix the fish sauce, rice vinegar, and sugar in a small container; set aside.
2. In a wok or big frying pan, heat the oil on moderate to high heat. Put in the eggs and stir-fry until scrambled.
3. Put in the green onions, garlic, and pepper flakes and continue to stir-fry for fifteen seconds or until aromatic.
4. Put in the carrots and bean sprouts; stir-fry until the carrots start to tenderize, approximately 2 minutes.
5. Put in the rice and cook for two to three minutes or until thoroughly heated.
6. Mix in the fish sauce mixture and put in the fried rice, tossing until uniformly coated.
7. To serve, decorate the rice with chopped mint, or cilantro, and chopped peanuts.

Yield: Servings 4–6

FLAVORFUL STEAMED RICE

Ingredients:

- ¼ cup chicken or vegetable broth
- ½ cup finely chopped cilantro
- ¾ cup long-grained rice
- 1 tablespoon minced gingerroot
- 1 teaspoon fish sauce
- 1 teaspoon salt
- 2 cloves garlic, minced
- 2 green onions, trimmed and thinly cut
- 2 teaspoons lime juice

Directions:

1. Bring a pot of water to a rolling boil. Put in the rice, allow the water to return to its boiling point, and cook for about ten minutes. Drain in a sieve, wash, and save for later. (Leave the rice in the sieve.)

2. Put in 1 inch of water to the pot and bring to its boiling point. Set the sieve over the boiling water, cover it using a clean kitchen towel and a lid, and allow to steam for approximately twenty minutes. (Check once in a while, putting in more water if required.)
3. Mash together the garlic and the salt to make a paste.
4. In a big container, mix the garlic paste, broth, gingerroot, green onions, lime juice, and fish sauce.
5. Put in the steamed rice and toss until well blended. Allow to cool to room temperature.
6. Mix the cilantro into the rice.

Yield: Servings 2–4

FRAGRANT BROWN RICE

Ingredients:

- 1 cups brown rice (white rice can be substituted)
- 1 kaffir lime leaf or 2 (2-inch-long, -½inch-wide) pieces of lime zest
- 1 medium carrot, peeled and julienned
- 1 tablespoon finely chopped gingerroot
- 1 tablespoon lime juice
- 1½ stalks celery, trimmed and thinly cut
- 2 garlic cloves, minced
- 2 red chili peppers, seeded and minced
- 2 tablespoons vegetable oil
- 4 green onions, trimmed and thinly cut
- 4½–5½ cups vegetable stock
- Salt and freshly ground pepper to taste

Directions:

1. In a moderate-sized to big deep cooking pan, heat the vegetable oil on medium. Put in the garlic and green onions, and cook for a couple of minutes. Put in the celery, carrots, chilies, and ginger, and cook for another two minutes.

2. Put in the rice and stir until well blended. Put in half of the vegetable stock, the kaffir lime leaf, lime juice, and salt and pepper. Bring to its boiling point; decrease the heat and simmer, uncovered, for fifty minutes, putting in additional stock as required.

Yield: Servings 4–6

FRAGRANT WHITE RICE

Ingredients:

- 1 stalk lemongrass, cut into thin rings (inner soft potion only)
- 10 fresh curry leaves
- 1¼ cups coconut milk
- 1¾ cups water
- 2 mace blades
- 2 tablespoons vegetable oil
- 2½ cups Jasmine rice
- 6 cloves
- Salt and freshly ground pepper to taste
- Zest of ½ kaffir lime

Directions:

1. In a moderate-sized-large deep cooking pan, heat the oil on medium. Put in the curry leaves and sautée. until you can start to smell the aroma. Put in the lime zest and the rest of the spices and sautée. for another two to three minutes, stirring continuously.
2. Put in the rice to the pot and stir until blended with the spice mixture. Put in the water, coconut milk, and salt and pepper. Bring to its boiling point; reduce heat, cover, and simmer for fifteen to twenty minutes or until the liquids have been absorbed. Adjust seasoning.

Yield: Servings 6–8

FRIED RICE WITH CHINESE OLIVES

Ingredients:

- ½ cup ground pork or chicken
- 10 Chinese olives, pitted and chopped
- 3 cloves garlic, minced
- 3 cups day-old cooked rice Fish sauce (not necessary)
- 3 tablespoons vegetable oil
- Chopped cilantro
- Cucumber slices
- Hot sauce
- Lime wedges

Directions:

1. Heat the oil in a wok or big frying pan on medium. Put in the garlic and stir-fry for a short period of time. Put in the pork and olives. Stir-fry until the pork is thoroughly cooked and any juices that have collected have cooked off.
2. Put in the rice, breaking up any clumps, and stir-fry until the rice is hot. Adjust the saltiness with a small amount of fish sauce if required.
3. Serve accompanied by cucumber slices, lime wedges, chopped cilantro, and hot sauce.

Yield: Servings 2–3

FRIED RICE WITH PINEAPPLE AND SHRIMP

Ingredients:

- ½ teaspoon curry powder
- ½ teaspoon shrimp paste
- ½ teaspoon turmeric
- 1 cup finely chopped onion
- 1 ripe whole pineapple
- 2 garlic cloves, thoroughly minced 10 ounces peeled shrimp, deveined and slice into ½-inch pieces
- 2¼ cups day-old, cooked Jasmine or other long grained rice

- 4 tablespoons vegetable oil
- Salt to taste
- Sugar to taste

Directions:

1. To prepare the pineapple, cut it in half along the length, leaving the leaves undamaged on 1 side. Scoop out the pineapple flesh of both halves, leaving a ½-inch edge on the half with the leaves. Reserve the hollowed-out half to use as a serving container. Dice the pineapple fruit and save for later.
2. Preheat your oven to 350 degrees.
3. In a wok or heavy sauté pan, heat the oil on medium. Put in the onion and garlic, and sauté until the onion is translucent. Using a slotted spoon, remove the onions and garlic from the wok and save for later.
4. Put in the shrimp and sauté roughly one minute; remove and save for later.
5. Put in the turmeric, curry powder, and shrimp paste to the wok; stir-fry for a short period of time. Put in the rice and stir-fry for two to three minutes. Put in the pineapple and carry on cooking. Put in the reserved shrimp, onions, and garlic. Season to taste with salt and sugar.
6. Mound the fried rice into the pineapple "serving container." Put the pineapple on a baking sheet and bake for roughly ten minutes. Serve instantly.

Yield: Servings 2–4

FRIED RICE WITH TOMATOES

Ingredients:

- 1 clove garlic, minced
- 1 green onion, trimmed and cut
- 1 medium onion, slivered
- 1 teaspoon fish sauce
- 1 teaspoon ground white pepper
- 1 teaspoon sugar
- 1 tomato, cut into 8–10 wedges

- 1 whole boneless, skinless chicken breast, cut into bitesized pieces
- 2 eggs
- 2 teaspoons soy sauce
- 3 tablespoons vegetable oil
- 4 cups cooked rice

Directions:

1. In a big frying pan or wok, heat the vegetable oil on moderate to high. Put in the chicken pieces and the garlic, and stir-fry one minute.
2. Put in the onion and continue to stir-fry for another minute.
3. Break in the eggs, stirring thoroughly.
4. Mix in all the rest of the ingredients; stir-fry for two more minutes.
5. Serve instantly.

Yield: Servings 2–4

GINGER RICE

Ingredients:

- 1 (½-inch) piece of gingerroot, peeled and thinly cut
- 1 red chili pepper, seeded and minced
- 1 stalk lemongrass, cut into rings (soft inner portion only)
- 1½ cups long-grained rice
- 2 tablespoons vegetable oil
- 2¾ cups water
- 2—3 green onions, cut into rings
- Juice of ½ lime
- Pinch of brown sugar
- Pinch of salt

Directions:

1. In a moderate-sized-sized pot, heat the oil on moderate heat. Put in the gingerroot, lemongrass, green onions, and chili pepper; sautée. for two to three minutes.
2. Put in the rice, brown sugar, salt, and lime juice, and continue to sautée. for another two minutes. Put in the water to the pot and bring to its boiling point.
3. Reduce the heat, cover with a tight-fitting lid, and simmer for fifteen to twenty minutes, until the liquid is absorbed.

Yield: Servings 4–6

LEMON RICE

Ingredients:

- ¼ cup cashew nuts, soaked in cold water for five minutes
- ¼ teaspoon mustard seed
- ½ teaspoon turmeric
- 1 cup basmati rice, soaked in cold water for thirty minutes
- 1 cups water Pinch of salt
- 1 green chili pepper, seeded and minced
- 1 tablespoon vegetable oil
- 8 fresh curry leaves
- Juice of ½ lemon

Directions:

1. In a moderate-sized-sized pan, bring the water to its boiling point. Put in the salt, rice, and turmeric; reduce heat, cover, and simmer for about ten minutes. (At the end of the ten minutes, the rice will have absorbed all of the liquid.) Turn off the heat and allow to cool.
2. In a wok, heat the oil and stir-fry the chili pepper. Put in the nuts, mustard seed, and curry leaves; carry on cooking for another half a minute. Mix in the lemon juice. Put in the cooled rice to the wok and toss until heated.

Yield: Servings 2–4

SHRIMP RICE

Ingredients:

- 1 ¾cups long-grained rice
- 1 medium to big onion, finely chopped
- 1 quart water
- 1 stalk lemongrass, halved and crushed (inner white potion only)
- 1 tablespoon lime juice
- 2 cloves garlic, finely chopped
- 2 red chili peppers, seeded, veined, and thoroughly minced
- 4 tablespoons fish sauce
- 5 tablespoons dried shrimp, soaked in cold water for about ten minutes
- 5 tablespoons vegetable oil
- Salt to taste

Directions:

1. Make a shrimp paste by combining the dried shrimp, chili peppers, onion, and garlic in a blender or food processor and processing until the desired smoothness is achieved.
2. In a moderate-sized-sized deep cooking pan, warm the oil on moderate heat. Put in the shrimp paste and cook for three to four minutes, stirring continuously.
3. Put in the fish sauce, lime juice, and salt to the paste and stir until well mixed; set aside.
4. Pour the rice into a big pot and put the lemongrass on top. Put in the water and bring to its boiling point; reduce heat, cover, and simmer for fifteen minutes.
5. Take away the lemongrass stalk and mix in the shrimp paste. Carry on cooking for five to ten minutes or until the rice is done.

Yield: Servings 4–6

SWEET-SPICED FRIED RICE

Ingredients:

- ½ teaspoon mace

- 1 (1-inch) cinnamon stick
- 1 bay leaf
- 1 tablespoon brown sugar
- 1½ cups long-grained rice (such as Jasmine)
- 2¼ cups water
- 3 cloves
- 3 tablespoons vegetable oil ½ onion, cut into rings
- Salt

Directions:

1. Soak the rice in cold water for about twenty minutes.
2. In the meantime, heat the oil in a moderate-sized pot on moderate heat. Put in the onions and sauté until golden, roughly ten to fifteen minutes.
3. Put in the spices and sauté for another two minutes. Drizzle the brown sugar over the onion mixture and caramelize for one to two minutes, stirring continuously. Put in the rice and sautée. for another three minutes, stirring continuously.
4. Put in the salt and the water to the pot and bring to its boiling point. Decrease the heat, cover, and simmer until the rice is soft, roughly ten to fifteen minutes.
5. Take away the cinnamon stick and cloves before you serve.

Yield: Approximately 4 cups

VEGETARIAN FRIED RICE

Ingredients:

- ½ cup finely diced onion
- ½ cup vegetable stock
- ½ teaspoon brown sugar
- ½ teaspoon ground turmeric
- 1 tablespoon finely chopped fresh gingerroot
- 2 garlic cloves, finely chopped
- 2 medium carrots, peeled and julienned into 1-inch pieces

- 2 red chili peppers, seeded, veined, and thinly cut
- 2 stalks of celery, cut
- 2 tablespoons vegetarian "oyster" sauce
- 3 cups day-old long-grained rice
- 3 tablespoons soy sauce
- 3 tablespoons vegetable oil, divided
- 4 scallions, cut
- 7 ounces green beans, trimmed and slice into 1-inch pieces
- 9 ounces tomatoes, peeled, seeded, and diced
- Grated zest and juice of ½ of a lime
- Salt and freshly ground pepper to taste

Directions:

1. In a wok or big sauté pan, heat 2 tablespoons of the vegetable oil on moderate to high heat. Put in the rice and stir-fry for two to three minutes. Take away the rice from the wok and save for later.
2. Put in the remaining tablespoon of oil to the wok. Put in the onion, garlic, and ginger; sauté for a minute.
3. Put in the chilies, scallions, green beans, carrots, and celery; stir-fry for about three minutes.
4. Put in the stock and bring to its boiling point; decrease the heat and simmer for five minutes.
5. Put in the tomatoes and simmer for another two minutes.
6. Put in the "oyster" and soy sauces and turmeric. Sprinkle salt and pepper to taste.
7. Mix in the lime zest, lime juice, brown sugar, and rice. Mix until blended.

Yield: Servings 4–6

DESSERTS

BANANA COCONUT SOUP

Ingredients:

- 1 cinnamon stick
- 1 tablespoon lemon juice
- 2 tablespoons minced gingerroot
- 4 cups banana slices, plus extra for decoration
- 4 cups canned coconut milk
- Salt to taste

Directions:

1. In a big deep cooking pan, bring the coconut milk to its boiling point. Put in the banana, ginger, cinnamon stick, lemon juice, and a pinch of salt. Decrease the heat and simmer for ten to fifteen minutes or until the banana is very tender.
2. Take away the cinnamon stick and let cool slightly.
3. Using a handheld blender (or a blender or food processor), purée the soup until the desired smoothness is achieved.
4. Serve the soup in preheated bowls, decorated with banana slices and coconut.

Yield: Servings 6–8

BANANAS POACHED IN COCONUT MILK

Ingredients:

- ¼ teaspoon salt
- 1 cup sugar
- 2–3 small, slightly green bananas
- 4 cups coconut milk

Directions:

1. Peel the bananas and slice them in half along the length.
2. Pour the coconut milk into a pan big enough to hold the bananas laid flat in a single layer. Put in the sugar and salt and bring to its boiling point.
3. Reduce the heat, put in the bananas, and simmer until the bananas are just warmed through, approximately 3 to five minutes.
4. Serve the bananas warm on small plates decorated with fresh coconut and pineapple wedges.

Yield: Servings 2–3

CITRUS FOOL

Ingredients:

- ½ cup heavy cream
- ½ cup orange, lime, or lemon juice
- 1 big egg, beaten
- 2 (3-inch-long, ½-inch wide) strips of citrus zest, minced
- 3 tablespoons sugar
- 3 tablespoons unsalted butter

Directions:

1. Put the juice in a small deep cooking pan. Over moderate to high heat, reduce the liquid by half.
2. Take away the pan from the heat and mix in the sugar and butter. Mix in the egg until well blended.
3. Return the pan to the burner and cook on medium-low heat for three to five minutes or until bubbles barely start to form.
4. Take away the pan from the heat and mix in the citrus zest. Put the pan in a container of ice and stir the mixture until it is cold.
5. In another container, whip the cream until firm. Fold the citrus mixture meticulously into the cream.

Yield: Servings 4

COCONUT CUSTARD

Ingredients:

- 1 (16-ounce) can coconut cream
- 3 tablespoons butter
- 6 big eggs, lightly beaten
- 1 cup fine granulated sugar
- Fresh tropical fruit (not necessary)

Directions:

1. In a large, heavy-bottomed deep cooking pan, mix together the coconut cream and the sugar.
2. Over moderate heat, cook and stir the mixture until the sugar is thoroughly blended.
3. Lower the heat to low and mix in the eggs. Cook while stirring once in a while, until the mixture is thick and coats the back of a spoon, approximately ten to twelve minutes.
4. Take away the pan from the heat and put in the butter. Stir until the butter is completely melted and blended.
5. Pour the custard into six 4-ounce custard cups. Put the cups in a baking pan. Pour boiling water into the baking pan until it comes midway up the sides of the custard cups.
6. Cautiously move the baking pan to a preheated 325-degree oven. Bake the custards for thirty to forty minutes until set. (The tip of a knife should come out clean when inserted into the middle of the custard.)
7. Serve warm or at room temperature. Decorate using chopped tropical fruit, if you wish.

Yield: Servings 6

COCONUT-PINEAPPLE SOUFFLÉ FOR 2

Ingredients:

- ½ cup (½-inch) cubes ladyfingers or sponge cake

- 1 egg yolk
- 2 egg whites
- 2 tablespoons dark rum
- 2 tablespoons finely chopped fresh pineapple
- 2 tablespoons sugar
- 2½ tablespoons grated sweetened coconut
- Lemon juice
- Softened butter for the molds
- Sugar for the molds

Directions:

1. Preheat your oven to 400 degrees.
2. Butter 2-¾ or 1-cup soufflée molds and then drizzle them with sugar. Place in your fridge the molds until ready to use.
3. Put the ladyfinger cubes in a small container. Pour the rum over the cubes and allow to soak for five minutes.
4. Squeeze the juice from the pineapple, saving both the pulp and 1 tablespoon of the juice.
5. In a small container, beat the egg yolk with the pineapple juice until very thick. Fold in the cake cubes, pineapple pulp, and coconut.
6. In another small container, beat the egg whites with a few drops of lemon juice until foamy. Slowly put in the 2 tablespoons of sugar, while continuing to beat until the whites are stiff and shiny.
7. Lightly fold the pineapple mixture into the egg whites.
8. Ladle the batter into the prepared molds and bake for eight to ten minutes or until puffy and mildly browned.

Yield: 2

CRISPY CREPES WITH FRESH FRUIT

Ingredients:

- ¼ cup shredded, unsweetened coconut
- 1 cup heavy cream

- 1 package frozen puff pastry sheets, thawed in accordance with package instructions
- 1 tablespoon unflavored rum or coconut-flavored rum
- 2 cups raspberries, blueberries, or other fresh fruit, the best 12 berries reserved for decoration
- 2 tablespoons confectioner's sugar, divided

Directions:

1. Preheat your oven to 400 degrees.
2. Put the puff pastry sheet on a work surface and slice into 12 equalsized pieces. Put the pastry pieces on a baking sheet.
3. Bake the pastry roughly ten minutes. Take out of the oven and use a sifter to shake a small amount of the confectioner?s sugar over the puff pastry. Return to the oven and carry on baking for roughly five minutes or until golden. Put the puff pastry on a wire rack and let cool completely.
4. Put the berries in a food processor and for a short period of time process to make a rough purée.
5. Whip the cream with the rest of the confectioner's sugar until thick, but not firm. Mix in the coconut and the rum.
6. To serve, place 1 piece of puff pastry in the center of each serving plate, spoon some cream over the pastry, and then top with some purée. Put another pastry on top, decorate with some of the rest of the berries, any remaining juice from the purée, and a drizzle of confectioner's sugar.

FRESH ORANGES IN ROSE WATER

Ingredients:

- 1½ cups sugar
- 3 cups water
- 4–6 teaspoons rose water
- 8 oranges

Directions:

1. Peel and segment the oranges. Put them in a container, cover, and set aside in your fridge.
2. In a deep cooking pan, bring the water and the sugar to its boiling point over moderatehigh heat. Boil gently for fifteen to 20 or until the mixture becomes syrupy. Turn off the heat and mix in the rose water. Allow to cool to room temperature and then place in your fridge
3. To serve, place orange segments in individual dessert cups. Pour rose water syrup over the top.

Yield: Servings 6–8

LEMONGRASS CUSTARD

Ingredients:

- ½ cup suga
- 2 cups whole milk
- 2 stalks fresh lemongrass, finely chopped (soft inner portion only)
- 6 egg yolks

Directions:

1. Preheat your oven to 275 degrees.
2. In a moderate-sized-sized deep cooking pan, on moderate to high heat, bring the milk and the lemongrass to its boiling point. Lower the heat and simmer for five minutes. Cover the milk mixture, remove the heat, and allow it to sit for about ten minutes on the burner.
3. In a mixing container, beat the egg yolks with the sugar until thick.
4. Strain the milk mixture through a fine-mesh sieve, then slowly pour it into the egg yolks, whisking continuously.
5. Split the mixture between 6 small custard cups and put the cups in a high-sided baking or roasting pan. Put in warm water to the pan so that it reaches to roughly an inch below the top of the custard cups. Cover the pan firmly using foil.
6. Put the pan in your oven and bake for roughly twenty minutes or until the custards are set on the sides but still slightly wobbly in the middle.

Yield: Servings 6

MANGO FOOL

Ingredients:

- ¼ cup sugar
- 1 cup heavy cream
- 1 tablespoon confectioners' sugar
- 2 ripe mangoes, peeled and flesh cut from the pits 2 tablespoons lime juice
- Crystallized ginger (not necessary)
- Mint leaves (not necessary)

Directions:

1. Put the mangoes in a food processor with the lime juice and sugar. Puréee until the desired smoothness is achieved.
2. In a big container beat the heavy cream with the confectioners' sugar until firm.
3. Thoroughly fold the mango purée into the heavy cream.
4. Serve in goblets decorated with crystallized ginger or sprigs of mint, if you wish.

Yield: Servings 4–6

MANGO SAUCE OVER ICE CREAM

Ingredients:

- 1 banana, peeled and chopped
- 1 tablespoon brandy (not necessary)
- 2 mangoes, peeled, pitted, and diced
- 1 cup (or to taste) sugar
- Juice of 2 big limes (or to taste)
- Vanilla ice cream

Directions:

1. In a moderate-sized-sized deep cooking pan using low heat, simmer the mangoes, banana, sugar, and lime juice for thirty minutes, stirring regularly.
2. Put in the brandy and simmer 5 more minutes.
3. Turn off the heat and let cool slightly or to room temperature.
4. To serve, scoop ice cream into individual serving bowls. Ladle sauce over top.

Yield: 2 cups

PINEAPPLE RICE

Ingredients:

- ¼ cup sugar
- ½ cup short-grained rice
- 1 ripe pineapple
- 2 teaspoons chopped crystallized ginger, divided
- 3 tablespoons roasted cashew nuts, chopped
- Pinch of salt
- Zest and juice of 1 lemon

Directions:

1. Chop the pineapple in half along the length, leaving the leaves undamaged on 1 side. Scoop out the pineapple flesh of both halves, leaving a ½-inch edge on the half with the leaves. Dice the pineapple fruit from 1 half and purée the fruit from the other half in a food processor together with the sugar and salt; set aside.
2. Strain the fruit purée through a fine-mesh sieve into a measuring cup. Put in enough water to make 1¾ cups. Move to a small deep cooking pan and bring to its boiling point on moderate to high heat.
3. Wash and drain the rice. Mix the rice into the pineapple purée. Mix in the lemon zest, lemon juice, and 1 teaspoon of the ginger. Bring to its boiling point; reduce heat, cover, and simmer until the liquid has been absorbed, approximately twenty minutes.
4. Combine the reserved pineapple cubes into the rice.
5. To serve, spoon the rice into the hollowed out pineapple that has the leaves. Decorate using the rest of the ginger and the roasted cashews.

Yield: Servings 4–6

PINEAPPLE-MANGO SHERBET

Ingredients:

- ½ cup plain yogurt
- 1 big orange, peeled and segmented
- 1 cup pineapple pieces
- 1 tablespoon lime zest
- 1 teaspoon orange-flavored liqueur (not necessary)
- 2 mangoes, peeled, pitted, and slice into 1-inch cubes
- 1 cup sugar

Directions:

1. Put the orange segments, mango cubes, and pineapple pieces on a baking sheet lined with waxed paper; store in your freezer for 30 to forty-five minutes or until just frozen.
2. Move the fruit to a food processor. Put in the lime zest and sugar, and pulse until well blended.
3. While the machine runs, add the yogurt and liqueur. Process for another three minutes or until the mixture is fluffy.
4. Pour the mixture into an 8" × 8" pan, cover using foil, and freeze overnight.
5. To serve, let the sherbet temper at room temperature for ten to fifteen minutes, then scoop into glass dishes.

Yield: Servings 4–6

PUMPKIN CUSTARD

Ingredients:

- 1 small cooking pumpkin
- 5 eggs
- 1 cup brown sugar

Directions:

1. With a small sharp knife, cautiously chop the top off of the pumpkin.
2. Using a spoon, remove and discard the seeds and most of the tender flesh; set the pumpkin aside.
3. In a moderate-sized-sized mixing container, whisk the eggs together. Mix in the brown sugar, salt, and coconut cream until well blended.
4. Pour the mixture into the pumpkin.
5. Put the pumpkin in a steamer and allow to steam for roughly twenty minutes or until the custard is set.

Yield: Servings 4

PUMPKIN SIMMERED IN COCONUT MILK

Ingredients:

- ½ cup coconut milk
- ½ teaspoon salt
- 1 cup water
- 2 cups fresh pumpkin meat cut into big julienned pieces (acorn squash is a good substitute)
- 1 cup brown sugar

Directions:

1. Place the water and the coconut milk in a moderate-sized pan using low heat. Put in the salt and half of the sugar; stir until well blended. Adjust the sweetness to your preference by put in more water or sugar if required.
2. Put in the julienned pumpkin to the pan and bring to its boiling point on moderate heat. Reduce to a simmer and cook until soft, approximately 5 to ten minutes depending on both the texture of the pumpkin and your own preference.
3. The pumpkin may be served hot, warm, or cold.

Yield: Servings 4

STEAMED COCONUT CAKES

Ingredients:

- ¼ cup all-purpose flour
- ½ cup coconut milk
- ½ cup grated sweet coconut
- ½ cup rice flour
- 4 tablespoons finely granulated sugar
- 5 eggs
- Pinch of salt

Directions:

1. In a big mixing container, beat the eggs and the sugar together until thick and pale in color.
2. Put in the rice flours and salt.
3. Beating continuously, slowly pour in the coconut milk. Beat the batter for 3 more minutes.
4. Bring some water to boil in a steamer big enough to hold 10 small ramekins. When the water starts to boil, put the ramekins in the steamer to heat for a couple of minutes.
5. Split the shredded coconut uniformly between all of the ramekins and use a spoon to compact it on the bottom of the cups.
6. Pour the batter uniformly between the cups. Steam for about ten minutes.
7. Take away the cakes from the cups the moment they are sufficiently cool to handle.
8. Serve warm or at room temperature.

Yield: 10 cakes

STICKY RICE WITH COCONUT CREAM SAUCE

Ingredients:

- 1 cup coconut cream
- 1 teaspoon salt

- 3 cups cooked Sweet Sticky Rice
- 4 ripe mangoes, thinly cut (or other tropical fruits)
- 4 tablespoons sugar

Directions:

1. For the sauce, put the coconut cream, sugar, and salt in a small deep cooking pan. Stir to blend and bring to its boiling point on moderate to high heat. Decrease the heat and simmer for five minutes.
2. To serve, position mango slices on each plate. Put a mound of rice next to the fruit. Top the rice with some of the sauce.

Yield: Servings 6

SWEET STICKY RICE

Ingredients:

- ½ cup granulated sugar
- ½ teaspoon salt
- 1 cups canned coconut milk
- 1½ cups white glutinous rice

Directions:

1. Put the rice in a container and put in enough water to completely cover the rice. Soak for minimum 4 hours or overnight. Drain.
2. Coat a steamer basket with wet cheesecloth. Spread the rice uniformly over the cheesecloth. Put the container over quickly boiling water. Cover and steam until soft, approximately twenty-five minutes; set aside.
3. In a moderate-sized-sized deep cooking pan, mix the coconut milk, sugar, and salt and heat on moderate to high. Stir until the sugar is thoroughly blended. Pour over the rice, stir until blended, and allow to rest for half an hour
4. To serve, place in small bowls or on plates. Decorate using mangoes, papayas, or other tropical fruit.

Yield: Servings 6

TARO BALLS POACHED IN COCONUT MILK

Ingredients:

- 1 cup brown sugar
- 1 cup cooked taro, mashed
- 1 cup corn flour
- 2 cups glutinous rice flour
- 4 cups coconut milk
- Fresh tropical fruit (not necessary)
- teaspoon salt

Directions:

1. In a big mixing container, mix the rice and the flours.
2. Put in the mashed taro and knead to make a tender dough.
3. Roll into little bite-sized balls and save for later.
4. In a moderate-sized to big deep cooking pan, heat the coconut milk using low heat.
5. Put in the brown sugar and the salt, stirring until blended.
6. Bring the mixture to a low boil and put in the taro balls.
7. Poach the balls for five to ten minutes or until done to your preference.
8. Serve hot in small glass bowls, decorated with tropical fruit.

Yield: Servings 6–12

TOFU WITH SWEET GINGER

Ingredients:

- 1 (2- to 3-inch) piece of ginger, peeled and smashed using the back of a knife
- 1 12-ounce package tender tofu
- 3 cups water
- 1 cup brown sugar

Directions:

1. Put the water, ginger, and brown sugar in a small deep cooking pan. Bring to its boiling point using high heat. Lower the heat to a simmer and allow the sauce to cook for minimum ten minutes. (The longer you allow the mixture to cook, the spicier it will get.)
2. To serve, spoon some of the tofu into dessert bowls and pour some sauce over the top. (This sauce is equally good over plain yogurt.)

Yield: 3 cups of sauce

TROPICAL COCONUT RICE

Ingredients:

- ¼ cup toasted coconut
- 1 cup coconut cream
- 2 cups short-grained rice
- 2 cups water

Directions:

1. Place the rice, water, and coconut cream in a moderate-sized deep cooking pan and mix thoroughly. Bring to its boiling point on moderate to high heat. Decrease the heat and cover with a tight-fitting lid. Cook for fifteen to twenty minutes or until all of the liquid has been absorbed.
2. Allow the rice rest off the heat for five minutes.
3. Fluff the rice and mix in the toasted coconut and fruit.

Yield: Servings 6–8

TROPICAL FRUIT WITH GINGER CREÈME ANGLAISE

Ingredients:

- (1-inch) pieces peeled gingerroot, slightly mashed
- 1 cup half-and-half

- 2 tablespoons sugar A variety of tropical fruits, cut
- 3 egg yolks

Directions:

1. In a small heavy deep cooking pan on moderate to low heat, bring the ginger and the half-and-half to a slight simmer. Do not boil.
2. Meanwhile, whisk together the eggs yolks and the sugar.
3. Slowly pour the hot half-and-half into the egg mixture, stirring continuously so that the eggs do not cook.
4. Pour the custard back into the deep cooking pan and cook on moderate to low heat, stirring continuously using a wooden spoon for five minutes or until slightly thickened.
5. Pour the crèmes anglaise through a mesh strainer into a clean container and let cool completely.
6. Pour over slices of your favorite tropical fruits.

Yield: 1½ cups

WATERMELON ICE

Ingredients:

- ½ cup sugar
- 1 (3-pound) piece of watermelon, rind cut away, seeded, and cut into little chunks (reserve a small amount for decoration if you wish)
- 1 cup water
- 1 tablespoon lime juice
- Mint sprigs (not necessary)

Directions:

1. Put the water and sugar in a small deep cooking pan and bring to its boiling point. Turn off the heat and let cool to room temperature, stirring regularly. Set the pan in a container of ice and continue to stir the syrup until cold.
2. Put the watermelon, syrup, and lime juice in a blender and purée until the desired smoothness is achieved.

3. Pour the puréee through a sieve into a 9-inch baking pan. Cover the pan using foil.
4. Put into your freezer the purée for eight hours or until frozen.
5. To serve, scrape the frozen purée with the tines of a fork. Ladle the scrapings into pretty glass goblets and decorate with a small piece of watermelon or mint sprigs.

Yield: Servings 6–8

DRINKS AND TEAS

FRESH COCONUT JUICE

Ingredients:

- 1 young coconut
- Ice
- Sprig of mint for decoration

Directions:

1. Using a meat cleaver, make a V-shaped slice on the top of the coconut.
2. Pour the juice over a glass of ice.
3. Decorate using a mint sprig.

Yield: Servings 1–2 depending on the size of the coconut.

GINGER TEA

Ingredients:

- ½-¾ cup sugar
- 1 big branch (roughly
- 8 cups water
- pound) of ginger, cut into long pieces

Directions:

1. Bring the water to its boiling point in a big pan. Put in the ginger, reduce heat, and simmer for ten to twenty minutes, depending on how strong you prefer your tea.
2. Take away the ginger and put in the sugar to taste, stirring until it is thoroughly blended.
3. Serve hot or over ice.

Yield: 8 cups

ICED SWEET TEA

Ingredients:

- 1 cup hot water
- 1 tablespoon sugar
- 1 tablespoon sweetened condensed milk
- 1 teaspoon milk
- 1–2 tablespoons Thai tea leaves
- Ice

Directions:

1. Place the sugar and sweetened condensed milk into a big glass.
2. Put the tea leaves into a tea ball and place it in the glass.
3. Put in the hot water. Allow to steep until done to your preferred strength.
4. Stir to dissolve the sugar and sweetened condensed milk.
5. Put in ice and top with milk.

Yield: slightly more than 1 cup.

LEMONGRASS TEA

Ingredients:

- ¼– cup sugar
- 1 cup lemongrass stalks, chopped
- 8 cups water

Directions:

1. Bring the water to its boiling point in a big pan. Put in the lemongrass, turn off the heat, and allow to steep for ten to twenty minutes, depending on how strong you prefer your tea.
2. Take away the lemongrass and put in the sugar to taste, stirring until it is thoroughly blended.

3. Serve hot or over ice.

Yield: 8 cups

MANGO BELLINI

Ingredients:

- ½ teaspoon lemon juice
- 1 teaspoon mango schnapps
- 2 tablespoons puréed mango
- Chilled champagne

Directions:

1. Put the mango purée, mango schnapps, and lemon juice in a champagne flute.
2. Fill the flute with champagne and stir.

Yield: 1 glass

ROYAL THAI KIR

Ingredients:

- 1–2 teaspoons creème de mango or mango schnapps
- Chilled dry champagne

Directions:

1. Pour the creème into a champagne flute and fill with champagne.

Yield: 1 glass

SUPER-SIMPLE THAI ICED TEA

Ingredients:

- 2 tablespoons sugar
- 1 cup hot water
- Ice
- 1–2 tablespoons Thai tea leaves

Directions:

1. Place the sugar into a big glass.
2. Put the tea leaves in a tea ball and place it in the glass.
3. Put in the hot water. Allow to steep until done to your preferred strength.
4. Stir to dissolve the sugar and put in ice.

Yield: Approximately 1 cup

THAI "MARTINIS"

Ingredients:

- 1 bottle coconut rum
- 1 bottle dark rum
- 1 bottle light rum
- 1 whole ripe pineapple
- 3 stalks lemongrass, trimmed, cut into 3-inch lengths and tied in a bundle

Directions:

1. Take away the pineapple greens and then quarter the rest of the fruit. Put the pineapple quarters and the lemongrass bundle in a container big enough to hold all of the liquor.
2. Pour the rums over the fruit and stir until blended. Cover the container and let infuse for minimum one week at room temperature.
3. Take away the lemongrass bundle and discard.
4. Take away the pineapple quarters and slice into slices for decoration.
5. To serve, pour some of the rum into a martini shaker filled with ice; shake thoroughly. Pour into martini glasses and decorate with a pineapple slice.

Yield: 3 quarts

THAI ICED TEA

Ingredients:

- 1 cup sugar
- 1 cup Thai tea leaves
- 1–1½ cups half-and-half
- 6 cups water
- Ice

Directions:

1. Bring the water to boil in a moderate-sized pot. Turn off the heat and put in the tea leaves, pushing them into the water until they are completely submerged. Steep roughly five minutes or until the liquid is a bright orange.
2. Strain through a fine-mesh sieve or coffee strainer.
3. Mix in the sugar until thoroughly blended.
4. Allow the tea to reach room temperature and then place in your fridge
5. To serve, pour the tea over ice cubes, leaving room at the top of the glass to pour in three to 4 tablespoons of half-and-half; stir for a short period of time to blend.

Yield: Approximately 8 cups

THAI LIMEADE

Ingredients:

- 1–½ cup sugar
- 1 cup lime juice, lime rinds reserved
- 8 cups water
- Salt to taste (not necessary)

Directions:

1. Mix the lime juice and the sugar; set aside.
2. Bring the water to boil in a big pot. Put in the lime rinds and turn off the heat. Allow to steep for ten to fifteen minutes. Take away the lime rinds.

3. Put in the lime juice mixture to the hot water, stirring to completely dissolve the sugar. Put in salt if you wish.
4. Serve over ice.

Yield: 9 cups

THAI-INSPIRED SINGAPORE SLING

Ingredients:

- ¼– cup pineapple juice Mint sprig (not necessary)
- 1 tablespoon cherry brandy
- 1 tablespoon lime juice
- 1 tablespoon orange liqueur
- 1 teaspoon brown sugar
- 2 tablespoons whiskey
- Dash of bitters

Directions:

1. Put all of the ingredients into a cocktail shaker and shake thoroughly to blend.
2. Serve over crushed ice and decorate with a sprig of mint if you wish.

Yield: 1 cocktail

TROPICAL FRUIT COCKTAIL

Ingredients:

- 1 small mango, papaya, banana, or other tropical fruit, peeled and roughly chopped (reserve a small amount for decoration if you wish)
- 1 tablespoon brown sugar
- 1 teaspoon grated ginger
- 1⁄ cups orange or grapefruit juice
- 1⁄ cups pineapple juice
- 1–½ cup (or to taste) rum

- 4 tablespoons lime or lemon juice

Directions:

1. Put the chopped fruit, lime juice, ginger, and sugar in a blender and process until the desired smoothness is achieved.
2. Put in the rest of the ingredients to the blender and pulse until well blended.
3. To serve, pour over crushed ice and garnish with fruit slices of your choice.

Yield: 3–4 cups

THAI-INSPIRED COOKING

ASIAN 3-BEAN SALAD

Ingredients:

- ½ teaspoon lime zest
- 1 (14-ounce) can black beans
- 1 (14-ounce) can garbanzo beans
- 1 (14-ounce) can red kidney beans
- 1 cup chopped cilantro
- 1 moderate-sized red onion, chopped
- 1 teaspoon minced jalapeño
- 3 cloves garlic, minced
- 3 tablespoons rice vinegar
- 4 tablespoons olive oil
- Salt and pepper to taste

Directions:

1. Put all the beans in a colander. Thoroughly wash under cool running water. Drain and save for later.
2. Mix together all the rest of the ingredients and pour over beans; stir until blended.
3. Place in your fridge overnight, stirring once in a while. Sprinkle with salt and pepper.

Yield: Servings 4–6

ASIAN CARROT STICKS

Ingredients:

- –¼ teaspoon cayenne pepper
- ½–½ teaspoons paprika
- ½–1 teaspoon Chinese 5-spice powder

- 1 pound thin carrots, peeled and slice into quarters along the length
- 2 cloves garlic, minced
- 2 tablespoons rice vinegar
- 3 tablespoons chopped cilantro
- 4 tablespoons olive oil
- 4 tablespoons water
- Salt and pepper to taste

Directions:

1. Put the carrots in a pan big enough to hold them easily.
2. Cover the carrots with water and bring to its boiling point using high heat. Drain the carrots and return them to the pan.
3. Put in the 4 tablespoons of water, the olive oil, and the garlic; bring to its boiling point, reduce to a simmer, and cook until just soft. Drain.
4. In a small container, mix together rest of the ingredients; pour over the carrots, tossing to coat.
5. Sprinkle salt and pepper to taste.
6. The carrots may be eaten instantly, but develop a richer flavor if allowed to marinate for a few hours.

Yield: Servings 4–6

ASIAN COUSCOUS SALAD

Ingredients:

- ½ cup vegetable oil
- 1 clove garlic, minced
- 1 moderate-sized red onion, chopped
- 1 packed cup basil
- 1 packed cup cilantro
- 1 packed cup mint
- 1 pound snow peas, trimmed

- 1 red bell pepper, cored, seeded, and chopped
- 1 yellow bell pepper, cored, seeded, and chopped
- 1–2 jalapeño chilies, seeded and finely chopped
- 2 tablespoons lemon juice
- 2¾ cups couscous
- 3 tablespoons lime juice
- 3½ cups boiling water, divided
- 5–7 green onions, trimmed and thinly cut
- Salt and freshly ground black pepper to taste

Directions:

1. Put the snow peas, peppers, onions, chilies, garlic, and couscous in a big container; toss to blend.
2. Pour 3 cups of the boiling water over the couscous mixture, cover firmly, and allow it to stand at room temperature for an hour.
3. Put in the remaining fi cup boiling water and all the rest of the ingredients to the couscous; toss together, cover, and allow it to stand for minimum 30 more minutes.
4. Sprinkle with salt and freshly ground black pepper.

Yield: Servings 8–10

ASIAN MARINARA SAUCE

Ingredients:

- 1 (1-inch) piece of ginger, peeled and minced
- 1 cup water
- 1 medium onion, chopped
- 1 pound chopped canned tomatoes with the juice
- 1 teaspoon salt
- 1 teaspoon sugar
- 1—3 serrano chilies, seeded and minced
- 2 tablespoons vegetable oil

Directions:

1. In a big deep cooking pan, heat the oil on moderate heat.
2. Put in the onion and ginger and sauté for a couple of minutes.
3. Put in the chilies and carry on cooking one minute more.
4. Mix in the water, tomatoes, salt, and sugar. Decrease the heat to low and simmer for minimum 30 minutes.

Yield: Approximately 2 cups

ASIAN RATATOUILLE

Ingredients:

- ½ teaspoon salt
- ½-inch cubes
- ¾ cup vegetable stock
- 1 cup cut mushrooms
- 1 onion, slivered
- 1 red bell pepper, cored, seeded, and julienned
- 1 tablespoon chopped cilantro
- 1 tablespoon cornstarch
- 1 tablespoon dry sherry
- 1 teaspoon minced garlic
- 1 teaspoon minced ginger
- 2 Japanese eggplants (approximately 1 pound), cut into
- 2 ribs of celery, cut
- 2 small zucchini, halved along the length and cut
- 2 tablespoons soy sauce
- 2 teaspoons Plum Dipping Sauce (Page 34)
- 3 tablespoons sesame oil
- 3 tablespoons vegetable oil

Directions:

1. Put the eggplant in a colander and drizzle with the salt. Allow to rest for half an hour
2. In a big ovenproof pot, heat the sesame oil on medium. Put in the celery, onion, and red bell pepper; sautée for five minutes. Take the vegetables out of the pan and save for later.
3. Put in the vegetable oil to the pot. Sauté the zucchini, mushrooms, and eggplant for five minutes. Mix in the celery, onion, and bell pepper and save for later.
4. In a small mixing container, whisk together the stock, soy sauce, sherry, and cornstarch. Pour over the vegetables and stir until blended.
5. Bake, covered, in a 350-degree oven for forty minutes.
6. Mix in the garlic, ginger, and plum sauce. Cover and carry on baking for another ten minutes.

Yield: Servings 6–8

ASIAN-INSPIRED CHICKEN AND WILD RICE SOUP

Ingredients:

- 1 tablespoon vegetable oil
- 1–2 garlic cloves, minced
- 2 tablespoons fish sauce
- 2 whole boneless, skinless chicken breasts, trimmed and slice into fine strips
- 2–3 teaspoons minced ginger
- 6 cups low-fat, low-salt chicken broth

Directions:

1. In a big soup pot, heat the oil on moderate to high. Put in the chicken strips and sauté for two to three minutes.
2. Put in the garlic and gingerroot and sauté for one more minute.
3. Mix in the fish sauce, broth, and rice. Bring to its boiling point; reduce heat, cover, and simmer for about ten minutes.
4. Put in the green onions and snow peas; simmer to heat through.
5. Adjust seasoning with salt and freshly ground white pepper to taste.

Yield: Servings 6–8

CHICKEN SALAD — 1

Ingredients:

For the dressing:

- ¼ cup vegetable oil
- ½; teaspoon (or to taste) salt
- 1 tablespoon soy sauce
- 2 tablespoons rice wine vinegar
- 2 teaspoons grated gingerroot
- Pinch of sugar

For the salad:

- 1 cup bean sprouts
- 1 medium head of Chinese cabbage, shredded
- 1 tablespoon toasted sesame seeds
- 2 cups chopped cooked chicken
- 3 green onions, trimmed and cut
- 4 ounces snow peas, trimmed

Directions:

1. Put the salad dressing ingredients in a small container and whisk vigorously to blend.
2. In a moderate-sized-sized container, mix the chicken, snow peas, green onions, and bean sprouts. Put in the dressing and toss to coat.
3. To serve, position the cabbage on a serving platter. Mound the chicken salad over the cabbage. Decorate using the sesame seeds.

Yield: Servings 4

CHICKEN SALAD — 2

Ingredients:

- ¼ cup chopped cilantro, plus extra for decoration
- ¼ pound rice sticks
- 1 cup cut scallions
- 1 tablespoon dry sherry
- 1 tablespoon soy sauce
- 1 tablespoon vegetable oil
- 1 teaspoon sesame oil
- 2 whole boneless, skinless chicken breasts
- 3 tablespoons hoisin sauce, divided
- 3 tablespoons peanuts, chopped
- 3 tablespoons sesame seeds, toasted
- 4 tablespoons lime juice
- Bibb or romaine lettuce leaves
- Peanut oil for frying

Directions:

1. Mix 1 tablespoon of the hoisin sauce, the soy sauce, and the sherry in a moderate-sized container. Put in the chicken breasts and marinate for twenty minutes to half an hour.
2. Heat the vegetable oil in a big frying pan on moderate to high heat. Put in the chicken breasts, saving for later the marinade. Brown the breasts on both sides. Put in the reserved marinade to the frying pan, cover, and cook on moderate to low heat until soft, approximately twenty minutes.
3. Allow the chicken to cool completely, then shred it into bite-sized pieces; set aside.
4. In a moderate-sized-sized container, mix the shredded chicken with the rest of the hoisin sauce, the lime juice, sesame oil, sesame seeds, peanuts, scallions, and cilantro. Put in the shredded chicken and stir to coat.
5. Put in roughly an inch of peanut oil to a big frying pan and heat on high until the oil is super hot, but not smoking.
6. Put in the rice sticks cautiously and fry for roughly 6 to 8 seconds or until puffed and golden; turn the rice sticks using tongs and fry for another 6 to 8 seconds. Take away the rice sticks to a stack of paper towels to drain.

7. Toss about of the rice sticks with the chicken mixture.
8. To serve, place a mound of salad on a lettuce leaf on the center of each plate. Top with the rest of the rice sticks and decorate with additional cilantro.

Yield: Servings 4–6

CHICKEN SALAD—3

Ingredients:

- ½ cup soy sauce
- ½ cup super slimly cut celery
- ½ teaspoon sesame oil (not necessary)
- 1 (¼-inch) piece ginger, peeled and minced
- 1 clove garlic, minced
- 1 cup cooked chicken meat
- 1 scallion, thinly cut
- 1 tablespoon sugar
- 1 teaspoon vegetable oil
- 2 tablespoons rice vinegar
- cups shredded bok choy

Directions:

1. In a moderate-sized-sized container, toss together the chicken, bok choy, celery, and scallion.
2. In a small container, meticulously whisk together the rest of the ingredients. Pour over the salad and toss thoroughly to blend.

Yield: 3–4 cups

CRAZY COCONUT PIE

Ingredients:

- ½ cup flour
- ¾ cup sugar
- ¾ stick of butter, melted
- 1 cup sweetened shredded coconut
- 1½ teaspoons vanilla
- 2 cups milk
- 4 eggs

Directions:

1. Preheat your oven to 350 degrees. Grease and flour a 10-inch pie plate.
2. Put all of the ingredients in a blender and blend for a minute. Pour the batter into the readied pan.
3. Bake for about forty-five minutes or until golden on top.

Yield: 1 (10-inch) pie

CREAM OF COCONUT CRABMEAT DIP

Ingredients:

- ¼ teaspoon salt 2 green onions, trimmed and thinly cut
- ¾ cup cream of coconut
- 1 jalapeño, seeded and minced
- 1 tablespoon lemon or lime juice
- 1¼ pounds (10 ounces) crabmeat, picked over to remove shell pieces
- 2 tablespoons chopped cilantro
- Ground white pepper to taste

Directions:

1. In a small deep cooking pan, mix the cream of coconut, crabmeat, and salt; bring to a simmer on moderate to low heat. Simmer for five minutes.
2. Mix in the green onions, cilantro, lemon juice, jalapeño, and pepper. Pour into a serving dish and allow it to stand at room temperature until cool.

3. Serve with fresh vegetables and crackers.

Yield: Approximately 2 cups

CRUNCHY SPROUT SALAD

Ingredients:

- ¼ cup rice vinegar
- 1 tablespoon sugar
- 2 cups sprouts of your choice
- 2 tablespoons fish or soy sauce
- 2 tablespoons vegetable oil
- 2 teaspoons grated gingerroot
- 6 cups baby greens (if possible an Asian mix)

Directions:

1. In a big container whisk together the vinegar, fish sauce, vegetable oil, sugar, and gingerroot.
2. Put in the sprouts, toss to coat, and let marinate for half an hour
3. Put in the greens and toss until well blended.

Yield: Servings 4

GRILLED LOBSTER TAILS WITH A LEMONGRASS SMOKE

Ingredients:

- 3–4 whole lemongrass stalks, bruised
- 6 (4–6 ounce) lobster tails
- Cracked black pepper
- Olive oil
- Salt to taste

Directions:

1. To prepare the lobster tails, lay each tail flat-side down (shell up). Using a sharp knife, cut through the shell and midway through the meat along the length. Use your fingers to pull the meat away from the membranes and the inner shell, then invert the meat until it sits on top of the shell instead of being surrounded by it.
2. Brush the lobster liberally with olive oil and drizzle with black pepper. Put the lemongrass stalks in a Tuscan herb grill.
3. Heat grill to moderate-high heat. Put the herb grill on the main grill grate and put the lobster tails on top, meat side up. Close the lid of the grill and cook for seven to eight minutes. (The shells must be bright red and the meat fairly firm.)
4. Flip the lobster tails over and carry on cooking for two to three minutes.
5. Drizzle with salt before you serve.

Yield: Servings 6

GRILLED STEAK WITH PEANUT SAUCE

Ingredients:

- 1 (2-pound) flank steak, trimmed
- 1 recipe of Peanut Dipping Sauce
- 1 recipe of Thai Marinade

Directions:

1. Swiftly wash the steak under cold water and pat dry. Put the steak in a big Ziplock bag together with the marinade. Flip the meat until it is thoroughly coated with the marinade on all sides. Place in your fridge overnight.(Allow the steak return to room temperature before cooking.)
2. Preheat a broiler or grill. Cook the steak, flipping over once and coating with the rest of the marinade, until done to your preference
3. Take away the meat from the grill, cover it using foil, and allow it to rest for five minutes to let some of the juices reabsorb. To serve, finely slice the steak across the grain. Pass the peanut sauce separately.

Yield: Servings 6

JICAMA, CARROT, AND CHINESE CABBAGE SALAD

Ingredients:

- ½ cup chopped cilantro
- ½ teaspoon prepared chili-garlic sauce
- 1 cup vegetable oil
- 1 teaspoon ground anise
- 2 big carrots, peeled and finely julienned
- 2 pounds jicama, peeled and finely julienned
- 2 tablespoons lime juice
- 3/4 pound Chinese cabbage, thinly shredded
- Salt and black pepper to taste

Directions:

1. Thoroughly mix the ground anise, cilantro, vegetable oil, lime juice, and chili-garlic sauce in a big mixing container.
2. Put in the vegetables and toss to coat.
3. Sprinkle with salt and pepper.

Yield: Servings 6–8

LIME BUTTER CAKE

Ingredients:

- ¼ teaspoon salt
- 1 cup milk
- 1½ cups sugar
- 2 sticks unsalted butter
- 3 cups cake flour
- 3 tablespoons lime juice
- 3 teaspoons baking powder
- 4 eggs, lightly beaten

- Grated peel of 1 lime
- Powdered sugar (not necessary)

Directions:

1. Preheat your oven to 325 degrees.
2. Sift together the cake flour, baking powder, and salt three times; set aside.
3. In the container of an electric mixer, beat the butter until creamy.
4. Slowly put in in the sugar, then beat at moderate speed for five minutes, scraping down the sides of the container every so frequently.
5. Put in the beaten eggs slowly and carry on beating for 5 more minutes. (The mixture will be thick and twofold in volume.)
6. Using a rubber spatula, progressively fold in ¼of the flour mixture into the batter. Then fold in of the milk. Repeat this pulse until all of the flour and the milk have been blended. (You will put in flour last.)
7. Fold in the lime peel and lime juice.
8. Pour the batter into a greased molded cake pan, smoothing the surface and slightly building up the sides.
9. Bake the cake for 45 to 55 minutes or until the top is golden and the sides are starting to pull away from the pan.
10. Take out of the oven and allow to cool for one to two minutes. Cautiously unmold.
11. Allow to cool to room temperature. Sprinkle with powdered sugar or serve with Ginger Anglaise Sauce.

Yield: 1 (12-inch) cake

MANY PEAS ASIAN-STYLE SALAD

Ingredients:

- ½ cup fresh green peas
- ½ cup snow peas
- 1 cup sugar snap peas
- 1 tablespoon brown sugar
- 1 tablespoon rice vinegar

- 1 tablespoon sesame oil
- 2 teaspoons sesame seeds, toasted
- 2 teaspoons soy sauce
- 6 cups pea shoots or other sweet baby lettuce

Directions:

1. Bring a big pot of water to its boiling point. Put in the sugar snap peas and boil for a couple of minutes. Put in the snow peas and green peas and boil for a minute more. Drain and wash in cold water. Pat dry using paper towels.
2. In a big container, meticulously mix the sesame seeds, vinegar, oil, sugar, and soy sauce. Put in the peas and the greens and toss to coat.

Yield: Servings 4

MARINATED MUSHROOMS

Ingredients:

- ¼ cup rice wine vinegar
- ½ cup water
- ¾ cup olive oil
- 1 whole serrano or jalapeño pepper
- 1½ pounds whole small white mushrooms
- 2 stalks lemongrass
- 3 (½-inch) pieces gingerroot
- 3 cloves garlic
- Juice of 1 lime

Directions:

1. Put all of the ingredients apart from the mushrooms in a big pot; bring to its boiling point, reduce heat, and simmer for ten to fifteen minutes.
2. Put in the mushrooms to the pot, stirring to coat.
3. Take away the pot from the heat and let cool completely, approximately 1 hour.

4. Place in your fridge for minimum 2 hours, if possible overnight.

Yield: 25–35

MERINGUES WITH TROPICAL FRUIT

Ingredients:

- 2 cups heavy cream, whipped
- 2 cups mixed fresh tropical
- 2 cups superfine sugar
- 6 egg whites
- Butter at room temperature to prepare baking dishes
- fruit, cut into bite-sized pieces

Directions:

1. Preheat your oven to 200 degrees. Butter pieces of parchment paper cut to line 2 baking sheets.
2. Put the egg whites in a cold container. Beat until tender peaks form Put in the sugar and carry on beating until firm.
3. Using a pastry bag, pipe 3- to 4 -inch circles of meringue onto the readied baking sheets.
4. Bake for 90 to 1twenty minutes or until they are dry, ensuring not to let the meringues turn color. If the meringues aren't dry after 2 hours of baking, turn the oven off and let the meringues sit in your oven overnight.
5. Allow the meringues to cool to room temperature. Fill a pastry bag with the whipped heavy cream. Pipe cream into the center of the meringues. Top with tropical fruit before you serve.

Yield: Approximately 24

PEANUT-POTATO SALAD

Ingredients:

- ¼ cup chopped cilantro
- ¼ cup chopped mint
- ¼ cup peanut butter
- ¾ cup mayonnaise
- 1 cup salted peanuts, crudely chopped, divided
- 1 moderate-sized red bell pepper, cored and chopped
- 2 stalks celery, cut
- 3 pounds peeled boiling potatoes
- 3 tablespoons rice vinegar
- 4 green onions, trimmed and cut
- Salt and pepper to taste

Directions:

1. Bring a big pot of water to its boiling point using high heat. Put in the potatoes and cook until soft. Drain and cool. Cut into ½-inch cubes.
2. In a big container, mix the potato cubes, ¾ cup of peanuts, red bell pepper, celery, green onion, cilantro, and mint.
3. In a small container, whisk together the mayonnaise, peanut butter, and vinegar. Sprinkle salt and pepper to taste.
4. Pour the dressing over the potato mixture and toss to coat. Place in your fridge for minimum 1 hour. Decorate using the rest of the peanuts before you serve.

Yield: Servings 8–10

PICKLED CHINESE CABBAGE

Ingredients:

- 1 tablespoon chopped cilantro
- 1 tablespoon chopped garlic
- 2 big shallots or 1 medium onion, chopped
- 3 pounds Chinese cabbage, cored, halved, and thinly cut
- 4 cups water

- 6 cups rice vinegar
- Salt and white pepper

Directions:

1. Put all of the ingredients apart from the cabbage in a big stew pot and bring to its boiling point. Decrease the heat and simmer for five minutes.
2. Bring the cooking liquid back to its boiling point and mix in the cabbage. Cover and cook the cabbage for three to five minutes.
3. Take away the pot from heat and let cool completely. Season to taste with salt and white pepper.
4. Place in your fridge for minimum 8 hours before you serve.

Yield: 3 pounds

SOUTHEAST ASIAN ASPARAGUS

Ingredients:

- 1 cup toasted peanuts
- 1 pound asparagus, trimmed and slice into two-inch pieces
- 1 tablespoon sesame oil
- 1 teaspoon fish sauce
- 1 teaspoon toasted sesame seeds

Directions:

1. Heat the sesame oil in a big frying pan on moderate to high heat. Put in the asparagus and sauté for about three minutes.
2. Put in the fish sauce, sesame seeds, and peanuts. Sauté for two more minutes or until the asparagus is done to your preference.

Yield: Servings 4

SOUTHEAST ASIAN BURGERS

Ingredients:

- ¼ cup chopped basil
- ¼ cup chopped cilantro
- ¼ cup chopped mint
- 1 clove garlic, minced
- 1 pound ground beef or ground turkey
- 1 teaspoon sugar (not necessary)
- 2 tablespoons lime juice
- 3 shakes Tabasco
- 3 tablespoons bread crumbs

Directions:

1. In a moderate-sized-sized mixing container, mix all the rest of the ingredients.
2. Use your hands to gently mix the ingredients together and form 4 patties.
3. Season each patty with salt and pepper.
4. Grill the patties to your preference, approximately five minutes per side for medium.

Yield: Servings 4

SPICY SHRIMP DIP

Ingredients:

- ½ serrano chili, seeded and minced
- ½ teaspoon grated lemon zest
- ½ teaspoon salt
- 1 tablespoon minced chives
- 5 tablespoons butter
- 8 ounces shrimp, cleaned and chopped
- Salt and freshly ground black pepper to taste

Directions:

1. In a moderate-sized-sized sauté pan, melt the butter on moderate heat. Mix in the chives, salt, chili pepper, and lemon zest; sauté for a couple of minutes.

2. Lower the heat to low and put in the shrimp; sauté for about three minutes or until opaque.

3. Move the mixture to a food processor and crudely purée. Sprinkle with salt and pepper.

4. Firmly pack the purée into a small container. Cover using plastic wrap, and place in your fridge for 4 hours or overnight.

5. To serve, remove the shrimp dip from the fridge and let it sit for five to ten minutes. Serve the dip with an assortment of crackers and toast points or some favorite veggies.

Yield: Approximately 1 cup

THAI CHICKEN PIZZA

Ingredients:

- ¼— cup peanut or hot chili oil
- ½ cup crudely chopped dry-roasted peanuts
- 1 cup chopped cilantro leaves
- 1 medium carrot, peeled and crudely grated
- 1 recipe Asian or Thai Marinade
- 1 unbaked pizza crust
- 1½ cups bean sprouts
- 1½ cups fontina cheese
- 1½ cups mozzarella cheese
- 2 whole boneless, skinless chicken breasts, cut in half
- 4 green onions, trimmed and thinly cut

Directions:

1. Put the chicken breasts in an ovenproof dish. Pour the marinade over the chicken, flipping to coat completely. Cover and place in your fridge for minimum 8 hours. Allow the chicken to return to room temperature before proceeding.

2. Preheat your oven to 325 degrees. Bake the chicken for thirty to forty minutes or until thoroughly cooked. Take away the chicken from the oven and let cool completely. Shred the chicken into minuscule pieces; set aside.
3. Prepare the pizza dough in accordance with package directions.
4. Brush the dough with some of the oil. Top the oil with the cheeses, leaving a ½-inch rim. Evenly spread the chicken, green onions, carrot, bean sprouts, and peanuts on top of the cheese. Sprinkle a little oil over the top.
5. Bake in accordance with package directions for the crust. Remove from oven, drizzle with cilantro, before you serve.

Yield: 1 large pizza

THAI PASTA SALAD

Ingredients:

- ¼ teaspoon ground ginger
- ½ teaspoon red pepper flakes
- 1 clove garlic, minced
- 1 cup bean sprouts
- 1 cup rice wine vinegar
- 1 tablespoon brown sugar
- 1 tablespoon soy sauce
- 1½ cups thinly cut Napa cabbage or bok choy
- 1½ cups thinly cut red cabbage
- 2 medium carrots, shredded
- 2 tablespoons vegetable oil
- 2 tablespoons water
- 3 green onions, trimmed and thinly cut
- 3 tablespoons smooth peanut butter
- 8 ounces dried bow tie or other bite-sized pasta

Directions:

1. Cook the pasta in accordance with package directions. Drain and wash under cold water. Put the pasta in a big mixing container and put in the green onions, carrots, and cabbage.
2. In a small mixing container, meticulously mix all the rest of the ingredients except the sprouts.
3. Pour the dressing over the pasta and vegetables; cover and place in your fridge for minimum 2 hours or overnight.
4. Just before you serve, throw in the bean sprouts.

Yield: Servings 8–12

THAI-FLAVORED GREEN BEANS

Ingredients:

- ½ cup chopped cilantro
- 1 rounded tablespoon shrimp paste
- 2 pounds French or regular green beans, trimmed and slice into bite-sized pieces
- 2 tablespoons vegetable oil
- 2 teaspoons minced garlic
- 3 tablespoons unsalted butter

Directions:

1. In a pot big enough to hold all of the beans, steam them until soft-crisp.
2. Drain the beans, saving for later cooking liquid. Cover the beans using foil to keep warm.
3. In a small container, whisk together the shrimp paste and vegetable oil.
4. In a big frying pan, melt the butter on moderate to high heat. Put in the garlic and sauté until golden. Mix in the shrimp paste mixture and 1 tablespoon of the reserved cooking liquid.
5. Put in the reserved green beans, stirring to coat. Cook until thoroughly heated.
6. Take away the pan from the heat and toss in the cilantro.

Yield: Servings 6–8

THAI-SPICED GUACAMOLE

Ingredients:

- 1 big plum tomato, seeded and chopped
- 1 small garlic clove, minced
- 1 tablespoon chopped onion
- 1 teaspoon chopped serrano or jalapeño chili
- 1 teaspoon grated gingerroot
- 1 teaspoon grated lime zest
- 1–2 tablespoons chopped cilantro
- 2 ripe avocados, pitted and chopped
- 4 teaspoons lime juice
- Salt and freshly ground black pepper to taste

Directions:

1. Put the avocado in a moderate-sized container. Put in the lemon juice and crudely mash.
2. Put in the rest of the ingredients and gently mix together.
3. Serve within 2 hours.

Yield: 2 cups

THAI-STYLE GRILLED PORK CHOPS

Ingredients:

- 1 cup fish sauce
- 2 (1-inch-thick) pork chops
- 2 tablespoons cream sherry
- 2 teaspoons brown sugar
- 2 teaspoons minced gingerroot
- 3 tablespoons rice vinegar
- garlic clove, minced

Directions:

1. In a small deep cooking pan, on moderate heat, bring the garlic, fish sauce, sherry, vinegar, brown sugar, and gingerroot to its boiling point. Turn off the heat and let cool to room temperature. (You can also put the marinade in your fridge to cool it.)
2. Put the pork chops in a plastic bag and pour in the marinade, ensuring to coat both sides of the chops. Allow the chops marinate at room temperature for fifteen minutes.
3. Pour the marinade into a small deep cooking pan and bring to a simmer on moderate to low heat. Cook for five minutes.
4. Grill the chops on a hot grill for five to six minutes per side for medium.
5. Serve the chops with the marinade sprinkled over the top.

Yield: Servings 2

REGIONAL CUISINES

5-SPICED VEGETABLES

Ingredients:

- ¼ teaspoon crushed red pepper flakes
- ½ — ¾ teaspoon Chinese 5-spice powder
- ½ cup orange juice
- 1 cup carrot slices
- 1 pound mushrooms, cut
- 1 small onion, halved and thinly cut
- 1 tablespoon cornstarch
- 1 tablespoon vegetable oil
- 1–2 cloves garlic, minced
- 2 tablespoons soy sauce
- 2 teaspoons honey
- 3 cups broccoli florets

Directions:

1. In a small container, mix the orange juice, cornstarch, 5-spice powder, red pepper flakes, soy sauce, and honey; set aside.
2. Heat the vegetable oil in a wok or frying pan on moderate to high heat. Put in the mushrooms, carrots, onion, and garlic. Stir-fry for roughly 4 minutes.
3. Put in the broccoli and carry on cooking an extra 2 to 4 minutes.
4. Mix in the sauce. Cook until the vegetables are done to your preference and the sauce is thick, roughly two minutes.
5. Serve over rice noodles, pasta, or rice.

Yield: Servings 4

ALMOND "TEA"

Ingredients:

- ¼–½ cup sugar
- ½ teaspoon ground cardamom
- 2 cups milk
- 2 ounces pumpkin seeds
- 3 cups water
- 3 ounces blanched almonds

Directions:

1. Process the almonds, pumpkin seeds, cardamom, and half of the water in a blender or food processor until the solids are thoroughly ground.
2. Strain the almond water through cheesecloth (or a clean Handi Wipe) into a container. Using the back of a spoon, press the solids to remove as much moisture as you can.
3. Return the almond mixture to the blender and put in the remaining water. Process until meticulously blended.
4. Strain this liquid into the container.
5. Mix the milk into the almond water. Put in sugar to taste.
6. Serve over crushed ice.

Yield: Servings 4–6

BANANA BROWN RICE PUDDING

Ingredients:

- ¼ cup water
- ½ teaspoon cinnamon
- ½ teaspoon nutmeg
- 1 (fifteen-ounce) can fruit cocktail, drained
- 1 cup skim milk
- 1 medium banana, cut

- 1 teaspoon vanilla extract
- 1½ cups cooked brown rice
- 2 tablespoons honey

Directions:

1. In a moderate-sized-sized deep cooking pan, mix the banana, fruit cocktail, water, honey, vanilla, cinnamon, and nutmeg. Bring to its boiling point on moderate to high heat. Lower the heat and simmer for about ten minutes or until the bananas are soft.
2. Mix in the milk and the rice. Return the mixture to its boiling point, decrease the heat again, and simmer for ten more minutes. Serve warm.

Yield: Servings 4–6

BASIC VIETNAMESE CHILI SAUCE

Ingredients:

- ½ teaspoon brown sugar
- 1 tablespoon lemon juice
- 1 tablespoon rice wine vinegar
- 2 cloves garlic, minced
- 2 dried red chilies, stemmed, seeded, and soaked in hot water until soft
- 2 tablespoons fish sauce

Directions:

1. Using a mortar and pestle, grind together the dried chilies and the garlic to make a rough paste.
2. Mix in the sugar until well blended. Mix in the rest of the ingredients.

Yield: Approximately ¼ cup

BEEF CAMBOGEE

Ingredients:

- ½ cup chopped peanuts
- 1 pound sirloin, trimmed, and slice into bite-sized pieces
- 2 cups bean sprouts
- 2–3 moderate-sized russet potatoes, peeled and slice into bite-sized pieces
- 5 cups Red Curry Cambogee (recipe on page 250)

Directions:

1. In a big deep cooking pan, bring the curry sauce to a simmer.
2. Put in the meat and potatoes and simmer until done to your preference, approximately twenty minutes to half an hour.
3. Decorate using the peanuts and bean sprouts.

Yield: Servings 4–6

CAMBODIAN BEEF WITH LIME SAUCE

Ingredients:

- 1 tablespoon sugar
- 1 teaspoon water
- 1½ pounds sirloin, trimmed and slice into bite-sized cubes
- 2 tablespoons lime juice
- 2 tablespoons soy sauce
- 2 tablespoons vegetable oil
- 2 teaspoons freshly ground black pepper, divided
- 5–7 cloves garlic, crushed

Directions:

1. In a container big enough to hold the beef, mix the sugar, 1 teaspoon of black pepper, soy sauce, and garlic. Put in the beef and toss to coat. Cover and let marinate for half an hour
2. In a small serving dish, mix the rest of the black pepper, the lime juice, and the water; set aside.
3. In a big sauté pan, heat the vegetable oil on moderate to high heat. Put in the beef cubes and sauté for about four minutes for medium-rare.

4. This dish may be served either as an appetizer or a main dish. For the appetizer, mound the beef on a plate lined with lettuce leaves with the lime sauce on the side. Use toothpicks or small forks to immerse the beef into the lime sauce. For a main dish, toss the beef with the lime sauce to taste. Serve with Jasmine rice.

Yield: Servings 4

CAMBODIAN-STYLE PAN-FRIED CHICKEN AND MUSHROOMS

Ingredients:

- ½ teaspoon grated ginger
- 1 cup water
- 1½ pounds chicken breasts and legs
- 2 tablespoons vegetable oil
- 2 teaspoons sugar
- 4 cloves garlic, crushed
- 6 ounces dried Chinese mushrooms

Directions:

1. Put the dried mushrooms in a container, cover with boiling water, and allow to soak for half an hour Drain the mushrooms and wash under cold water; drain again and squeeze dry. Remove any tough stems. Chop the mushrooms into bite-sized pieces; set aside.
2. Put the vegetable oil in a wok or big frying pan on moderate to high heat. Put in the garlic and the ginger and stir-fry for a short period of time.
3. Put in the chicken and fry until the skin turns golden.
4. Mix in the water and the sugar. Put in the mushrooms.
5. Lower the heat to low, cover, and cook until the chicken is soft, approximately 30 minutes.

Yield: Servings 4–6

CARDAMOM COOKIES

Ingredients:

- ½ cup fine sugar
- 1 cup fine semolina
- 1½ teaspoons ground cardamom
- 3 tablespoons all-purpose flour
- 4 ounces ghee

Directions:

1. Preheat your oven to 300 degrees.
2. In a big mixing container, cream together the ghee and the sugar until light and fluffy.
3. Sift together the semolina, all-purpose flour, and cardamom.
4. Mix the dry ingredients into the ghee mixture; mix thoroughly.
5. Allow the dough stand in a cool place for half an hour
6. Form balls using roughly 1 tablespoon of dough for each. Put on an ungreased cookie sheet and flatten each ball slightly.
7. Bake for roughly thirty minutes or until pale brown.
8. Cool on a wire rack. Store in an airtight container.

Yield: 2 dozen cookies

CHAPATI

Ingredients:

- 1 cup lukewarm water
- 1 tablespoon ghee or oil
- 1½ teaspoons salt
- 3 cups whole-wheat flour

Directions:

1. In a big mixing container, mix together 2½ cups of flour and the salt. Put in the ghee and, using your fingers, rub it into the flour and salt mixture.

2. Put in the lukewarm water and mix to make a dough. Knead the dough until it is smooth and elastic, approximately ten minutes. (Do not skimp on the kneading; it is what makes the bread soft.)
3. Form the dough into a ball and put it in a small, oiled container. Cover firmly using plastic wrap and allow it to rest at room temperature for minimum 1 hour.
4. Split the dough into golf ball–sized pieces. Using a flour-covered rolling pin, roll each ball out on a flour-covered surface to roughly 6 to 8 inches in diameter and -inch thick.
5. Heat a big frying pan or griddle on moderate heat. Put a piece of dough on the hot surface. Using a towel or the edge of a spoon, cautiously press down around the edges of the bread. (This will allow air pockets to make in the bread.) Cook for a minute. Cautiously turn the chapati over and carry on cooking for 1 more minute. Chapatis must be mildly browned and flexible, not crunchy. Take away the bread to a basket and cover using a towel. Repeat until all of the rounds are cooked.

Yield: Servings 6–8

CHILIED COCONUT DIPPING SAUCE

Ingredients:

- ¼ cup fresh coconut juice
- 1 serrano chili, seeded and minced
- 1 tablespoon lime juice
- 1 teaspoon rice wine vinegar
- 1 teaspoon sugar
- 2 cloves garlic, minced
- 2 tablespoons fish sauce

Directions:

1. Bring the coconut juice, rice wine vinegar, and sugar to its boiling point in a small deep cooking pan. Turn off the heat and allow the mixture to cool completely.
2. Mix in the rest of the ingredients.

Yield: Approximately 1 cup

CUCUMBER RAITA

Ingredients:

- 1 teaspoon salt
- 1½ cups plain yogurt
- 1–2 green onions, trimmed and thinly cut
- 2 seedless cucumbers, peeled and slice into a small dice
- 2 tablespoons fresh mint
- Lemon juice to taste

Directions:

1. Put the diced cucumbers in a colander. Drizzle with salt and allow it to sit in the sink for fifteen minutes to drain. Wash the cucumber under cold water and drain once more.
2. Mix the cucumber, yogurt, green onions, mint, and lemon juice to taste.
3. Cover and place in your fridge for minimum 30 minutes. Check seasoning, putting in additional salt and/or lemon juice if required.

Yield: Approximately 4 cups

FRUIT IN SHERRIED SYRUP

Ingredients:

- 1 orange, peeled and segmented
- 1½ cups kiwi slices
- 2 cups fresh pineapple chunks
- 2 tablespoons dry sherry
- 2 tablespoons sugar
- 2 teaspoons lemon juice
- 4 tablespoons water

Directions:

1. In a small deep cooking pan using high heat, boil the sugar and the water until syrupy. Turn off the heat and let cool completely. Mix in the lemon juice and sherry; set aside.
2. In a serving container, mix the orange segments, the pineapple chunks, and the kiwi. Pour the syrup over the fruit and toss to blend. Place in your fridge for minimum 1 hour before you serve.

Yield: Servings 4–6

GARAM MASALA

Ingredients:

- 1 tablespoon whole black peppercorns
- 1 teaspoon whole cloves
- 2 small cinnamon sticks, broken into pieces
- 2 tablespoons cumin seeds
- 2 teaspoons cardamom seeds
- 4 tablespoons coriander seeds

Directions:

1. In a small heavy sauté pan, individually dry roast each spice on moderate to high heat until they start to release their aroma.
2. Allow the spices to cool completely and then put them in a spice grinder and process to make a quite fine powder.
3. Store in an airtight container.

Yield: Approximately 1 cup

HAPPY PANCAKES

Ingredients:

- ¼ cup mixed, chopped herbs (mint, cilantro, basil, etc.)
- ¼ teaspoon salt

- ½ cup bean sprouts
- ½ cup finely cut straw mushrooms, washed and patted dry
- 1 cup rice flour
- 1 tablespoon vegetable oil
- 1 teaspoon sugar
- 1½ cups water
- 2 eggs, lightly beaten
- 3 ounces cooked salad shrimp, washed and patted dry
- Chili dipping sauce

Directions:

1. In a moderate-sized-sized container, whisk together the rice flour, water, eggs, salt, and sugar. Set aside and let the batter rest for about ten minutes.
2. Strain the batter through a mesh sieve to remove any lumps.
3. Put in the vegetable oil to a big sauté or omelet pan. Heat on high until super hot, but not smoking.
4. Pour the batter into the hot pan, swirling it so that it coats the bottom of the pan uniformly. Drizzle the mushrooms over the batter. Cover and allow to cook for a minute.
5. Drizzle the shrimp and bean sprouts uniformly over the pancake. Carry on cooking until the bottom is crunchy and browned.
6. To serve, chop the pancake into four equivalent portions. Drizzle with the chopped herbs. Pass a favorite dipping sauce separately.

Yield: Servings 4

HONEYED CHICKEN

Ingredients:

- ½ teaspoon Chinese 5-spice powder
- 1 (1-inch) piece ginger, peeled and minced
- 1 medium onion, peeled and slice into wedges
- 1 pound boneless, skinless chicken breasts, cut into bite-sized pieces

- 2 tablespoons fish sauce
- 2 tablespoons honey
- 2 tablespoons soy sauce
- 2 tablespoons vegetable oil
- 3–4 cloves garlic, thinly cut

Directions:

1. Mix the honey, fish sauce, soy sauce, and 5-spice powder in a small container; set aside.
2. Heat the oil in a wok on moderate to high. Put in the onion and cook until it just starts to brown.
3. Put in the chicken; stir-fry for three to four minutes.
4. Put in the garlic and ginger, and continue stir-frying for 30 more seconds.
5. Mix in the honey mixture and allow to cook for three to four minutes, until the chicken is glazed and done to your preference.

Yield: Servings 3–4

HOT NOODLES WITH TOFU

Ingredients:

- ½ pound Chinese wheat noodles
- ½ pound dried tofu, soaked in hot water for fifteen minutes and slice into 1-inch cubes
- ½ pound firm tofu, cut into 1-inch cubes
- ½ teaspoon yellow asafetida powder
- 1 bunch choy sum, chopped into 1-inch pieces
- 2 cups mung bean shoots or bean sprouts
- 3 tablespoons lemon juice
- 3 tablespoons minced ginger
- 3 tablespoons sambal oelek
- 3 tablespoons sesame oil
- 3 tablespoons soy sauce
- Vegetable oil for frying

Directions:

1. Cook the noodles firm to the bite in accordance with package directions. Wash under cold water and drain; set aside.
2. Heat approximately two inches of vegetable oil in a wok or big frying pan over moderate high heat. Put in the firm tofu cubes and deep-fry until golden. Using a slotted spoon, remove the tofu cubes to paper towels to drain; set aside.
3. Put in the dried tofu pieces and deep-fry them until they blister. Remove and drain using paper towels; set aside.
4. In another wok or frying pan heat the sesame oil using high heat. Put in the ginger and stir-fry one minute.
5. Put in the asafetida and choy sum, and stir-fry until tender.
6. Mix in the soy sauce, sambal oelek, and lemon juice. Put in the noodles and tofu pieces. Stir-fry until hot, approximately 2 minutes more.

Yield: Servings 4

INDIAN-SCENTED CAULIFLOWER

Ingredients:

- ½ medium to big head of cauliflower, separated into florets and slice into pieces
- ½ teaspoon Garam Masala
- ½ teaspoon turmeric
- 1 (2-inch) piece ginger, peeled and minced
- 1 clove garlic, minced
- 1 teaspoon mustard seeds
- 1 teaspoon salt
- 3 tablespoons vegetable oil
- 3 tablespoons water

Directions:

1. In a deep cooking pan big enough to easily hold the cauliflower, heat the vegetable oil on moderate to high heat. Put in the mustard seeds and fry until they pop. Put in the garlic and the ginger; stirring continuously, cook until the garlic just starts to brown.
2. Mix in the turmeric. Put in the cauliflower pieces and toss to coat with the spice mixture.
3. Put in the water, cover, and allow to steam for 6 to ten minutes or until done to your preference.
4. Pour off any surplus water and drizzle with the garam masala.

Yield: Servings 2–4

MANGO CHUTNEY

Ingredients:

- ½ ounce golden raisins
- ½ teaspoon black mustard seeds
- 1 cup water
- 1 tablespoon chopped ginger
- 1 tablespoon minced garlic
- 1 teaspoon cumin
- 1–2 red chili peppers, seeded and minced
- 2 big green mangoes, peeled and cut
- 2 cups sugar
- 2 cups white vinegar
- 2 teaspoons Garam Masala
- 3 teaspoons salt
- 4 ounces dried apricots or cherries

Directions:

1. Put all of the ingredients in a heavy-bottomed deep cooking pan. Heat to a simmer on moderate heat, stirring until the sugar dissolves.
2. Simmer for thirty minutes or until thick.
3. Seal in airtight jars.

Yield: Approximately 5–6 cups

MINTED VEGETABLES

Ingredients:

- ½ cup vegetable broth
- 1 medium onion, cut into 1-inch pieces
- 1 red bell pepper, seeded and slice into 1-inch pieces
- 2 teaspoons vegetable oil, divided
- 3 cups broccoli pieces
- 3 cups thinly cut red cabbage
- 3–4 tablespoons chopped mint
- 4 medium carrots, peeled and slice into thin slices
- Salt and pepper to taste

Directions:

1. In a big frying pan, heat 1 teaspoon of vegetable oil on moderate to high heat. Put in the carrot slices, onion, and bell pepper; sauté for five minutes.
2. Put in the remaining teaspoon of oil, the broccoli, the cabbage, and the vegetable broth. Continue to sauté until the vegetables are done to your preference, approximately ten minutes for soft-crisp.
3. Sprinkle salt and pepper to taste. Mix in the chopped mint.

Yield: Servings 6

MULLIGATAWNY SOUP

Ingredients:

- 1 (1½-inch) cinnamon stick
- 1 (14-ounce) can coconut milk
- 1 jalapeño, seeded and cut
- 1 tablespoon ground cumin

- 1 tablespoon vegetable oil
- 2 medium onions, peeled
- 2 tablespoons ground coriander
- 2 teaspoons salt
- 2 teaspoons whole peppercorns
- 3 cloves garlic, peeled
- 3 pounds chicken wings
- 4 whole cloves
- 4–5 cups cooked rice
- 5 cardamom pods, bruised
- 6 cups chicken broth
- 8–12 fresh curry leaves
- Lemon juice to taste

Directions:

1. Put the chicken wings in a big soup pot. Cover the chicken with cold water.
2. Stick the cloves into 1 of the onions and put the onion in the pot with the chicken.
3. Put in the garlic, jalapeño, cinnamon stick, peppercorns, cardamom, coriander, cumin, and salt; bring the mixture to its boiling point, reduce to a simmer, and cook for two to three hours.
4. Allow the stock come to room temperature. Take away the chicken pieces from the broth and chop the meat from the bones. Set aside the meat.
5. Strain the broth.
6. Thinly slice the rest of the onion.
7. In a big sauté pan, heat the oil on moderate to high heat. Put in the onion slices and sauté until translucent. Put in the curry leaves and the broth. Heat to a simmer and allow to cook for five minutes.
8. Put in enough water to the coconut milk to make 3 cups of liquid. Put in this and the reserved meat to the broth. Heat the soup, but do not allow it to boil. Season to taste with additional salt and a squeeze of lemon juice.
9. To serve, place roughly ½ cup of cooked rice on the bottom of each container. Ladle the soup over the rice.

Yield: Servings 8–10

OYSTER MUSHROOM SOUP

Ingredients:

- ½ pound oyster mushrooms, cleaned and separated if large
- ½ stalk lemongrass, outer leaves removed, inner core finely chopped
- 1 tablespoon Tabasco
- 1 teaspoon sugar
- 2 tablespoons lemon juice
- 2–3 serrano chilies
- 3 (2-inch-long, ½-inch wide) pieces lime zest
- 4 cups vegetable broth

Directions:

1. In a big deep cooking pan, bring the vegetable broth and the Tabasco to its boiling point. In the meantime, crush the chilies with a mallet to break them slightly open: A good whack will do it.
2. Put in all of the rest of the ingredients to the boiling broth, reduce the heat, and simmer until the mushrooms are cooked to your preference. Take away the chilies before you serve.

Yield: Servings 4

PENINSULA SWEET POTATOES

Ingredients:

- ¼ teaspoon salt
- 1 (14-ounce) can coconut milk
- 1 bay leaf
- 1 pound sweet potatoes or yams of varying varieties, peeled and slice into bite-sized pieces

- 1 teaspoon sugar

Directions:

1. Put the sweet potato pieces in a big deep cooking pan. Put in barely sufficient water to cover them, and bring to its boiling point. Put in the bay leaf and cook until the potatoes are tender. Take away the bay leaf and discard.
2. Mix in the sugar and salt. After the sugar has dissolved, remove the pan from the heat and mix in the coconut milk. Tweak the seasonings by putting in salt and/or sugar if required. Adjust the consistency by putting in more water and/or coconut milk.

Yield: Servings 4

PORK MEDALLIONS IN A CLAY POT

Ingredients:

- ½ teaspoon ground black pepper
- 1 clove garlic, minced
- 1 cup water
- 1 tablespoon Black Bean Paste (Page 10)
- 1 tablespoon cornstarch
- 1 tablespoon Tamarind Concentrate (Page 20)
- 1 teaspoon rice wine
- 1 teaspoon sesame oil
- 2 pork tenderloins, trimmed and slice into ½-inch slices
- 2 tablespoons light soy sauce
- 2 tablespoons oyster sauce
- 2 tablespoons sweet (dark) soy sauce
- 2 tablespoons vegetable oil

Directions:

1. Prepare the marinade by combining the oyster sauce, light and dark soy sauces, Black Bean Paste, sesame oil, rice wine, black pepper, garlic, and cornstarch in a moderate-sized container.
2. Put in the pork slices to the container of marinade and toss to coat completely. Cover the pork and let marinate at room temperature for half an hour
3. Heat the vegetable oil in a wok on moderate to high heat. Put in the marinated pork and stir-fry for three to four minutes.
4. Move the pork to a clay pot or other ovenproof braising vessel.
5. Mix together the tamarind and water; pour over the pork.
6. Bake the pork in a 350-degree oven for about ninety minutes, until super soft.

Yield: Servings 4

POTATO SAMOSAS

Ingredients:

For the crust:

- ½ teaspoon salt
- 1½ cups all-purpose flour
- 4 tablespoons butter, at room temperature
- Ice water
- Vegetable oil for deep frying

For the filling:

- ¼ pound sweet peas, thawed if frozen
- ½ teaspoon chili powder
- ½ teaspoon turmeric
- 1 tablespoon ghee (see note) or oil
- 1 teaspoon salt
- 1¼ pounds russet potatoes, peeled
- 2 jalapeños, seeded and thinly cut
- 2 teaspoons mustard seeds

- 3 tablespoons chopped mint
- Lemon juice to taste

Directions:

1. To make the pastry crust: In a big container, sift together the flour and the salt. Using a pastry cutter, chop the butter into the flour mixture.
2. Put in the ice water, 1 tablespoon at a time, until a firm dough is achieved. You will probably use 5 to 6 tablespoons of water total. Knead the dough for roughly five minutes or until it is smooth and elastic. Put the dough in an oiled container, cover using plastic wrap, and set it aside while making the potato filling.
3. To make the filling: Bring a big pan of water to its boiling point. Put in the potatoes and cook until fairly soft. Drain the potatoes and let them cool until they are easy to handle. Cut them into a small dice; set aside.
4. In a big frying pan, heat the ghee on moderate to high heat. Put in the mustard seeds and sauté until the seeds start to pop. Mix in the turmeric and the chili powder; cook for fifteen seconds. Mix in the potatoes, peas, salt, and jalapeño slices. (It is okay if the potatoes and the peas get a little smashed.) Turn off the heat, mix in the mint and lemon juice to taste, and save for later.
5. Roll the pastry until it is fairly thin (-inch thick). Cut roughly ten 6-inch circles from the dough. Cut each circle in half. Put a loaded tablespoon of filling in the middle of each half circle. Dampen the edges of the dough with cold water, fold the dough over on itself to make a triangle, and seal tightly.
6. To fry, put in roughly 3 inches of vegetable oil to a big deep cooking pan. Heat the oil using high heat until super hot, but not smoking. Put in the samosas to the hot oil a few at a time and deep-fry until a golden-brown colour is achieved. Using a slotted spoon, remove the samosas to a stack of paper towels to drain.
7. Serve the samosas with Tamarind Dipping Sauce.

Yield: 20 samosas

PUNJAB FISH

Ingredients:

- ¼ teaspoon cinnamon
- ¼ teaspoon saffron strands, toasted and crushed
- ½ cup plain yogurt
- 1 (1-inch) piece ginger, peeled and minced
- 1 clove garlic, chopped
- 1 medium onion, thinly cut
- 1 teaspoon black pepper
- 1 teaspoon salt
- 1 teaspoon turmeric
- 2 serrano chilies, seeded and minced
- 2 tablespoons almond slivers
- 2 tablespoons boiling water
- 2 teaspoons cardamom
- 2 teaspoons cumin
- 2–3 tablespoons vegetable oil
- 4–6 firm-fleshed fish fillets, roughly 1-inch thick
- Lemon juice
- teaspoon ground cloves

Directions:

1. Wash the fish with cold water and pat dry. Rub the fish with lemon juice.
2. Mix the salt, pepper, and turmeric; drizzle over the fish.
3. Heat one to 2 tablespoons of vegetable oil in a big frying pan using high heat. Brown the fish swiftly on each side. Take away the fish to a plate, cover, and save for later.
4. Put in the onion to the same pan and sauté until translucent and just starting to brown.
5. Put the cooked onion in a food processor together with the garlic, ginger, chilies, and almonds. Process to make a paste, putting in a small amount of water if required. Put in the cumin, cardamom, cinnamon, and clove; process to meticulously blend.
6. If required, put in additional vegetable oil to the frying pan to make about 2 tablespoons. Heat the oil over moderate. Put in the spice mixture and cook, stirring continuously, for approximately 2 minutes. Swirl a small amount of water in the food processor to remove any remaining spices and pour it into the pan; stir until blended.

7. Pour 2 tablespoons of boiling water into a small cup. Put in the toasted saffron and stir until blended. Pour the saffron water into the frying pan.
8. Mix in the yogurt. Heat to a simmer and allow the sauce to cook for five minutes.
9. Put in the fish to the sauce, flipping to coat. Cover and allow to simmer for roughly ten minutes or until the fish is done to your preference.

Yield: Servings 4–6

RED CURRY CAMBOGEE

Ingredients:

- 1 cup boiling water
- 2 tablespoons vegetable oil
- 4 cups Lemongrass Curry Sauce
- 4 dried Thai bird chilies, stemmed and seeded
- 4 tablespoons sweet paprika

Directions:

1. Break the dried chilies into pieces and put them in a small container. Cover with the boiling water and allow it to sit until soft, approximately fifteen minutes.
2. Put the chilies, their steeping water, and the paprika in a blender. Process to make a thin paste.
3. Heat the vegetable oil on moderate to high heat in a wok. Put in the chili paste and stir-fry until it starts to darken. Turn off the heat and save for later.
4. Put the Lemongrass Curry Sauce in a moderate-sized deep cooking pan. Mix in half of the chili paste and bring to its boiling point. Lower the heat and allow to simmer for five to ten minutes. Check the flavor of the sauce, putting in more chili paste if required.

Yield: Approximately 4½ cups

This Cambodian sauce is a hotter version of the Lemongrass Curry Sauce. It makes a great base for beef dishes.

LEMONGRASS CURRY SAUCE

Ingredients:

- 1 cup chopped lemongrass, inner core only
- 1 teaspoon minced ginger
- 1 teaspoon turmeric
- 1 jalapeño chili, stemmed and seeded
- 3 small shallots, crudely chopped
- 3 (14-ounce) cans coconut milk
- 3 (2-inch-long, ½-inch wide) pieces lime peel
- ¼ teaspoon salt
- 4–5 cloves garlic, chopped

Directions:

1. Put the lemongrass, garlic, ginger, turmeric, chili, and shallots in a food processor; process to make a paste.
2. Bring the coconut milk to its boiling point and put in the lemongrass paste, lime peel, and salt. Decrease the heat and allow to simmer for 30 to forty-five minutes. Take away the lime peel.

Yield: Approximately 4 cups

ROASTED DUCK, MELON, AND MANGO SALAD

Ingredients:

- ½ big cucumber, seeded and cut
- ½ roast duck, meat removed and shredded
- ½ teaspoon granulated salt
- ½ teaspoon sesame oil
- 1 cup cubed cantaloupe
- 1 cup cubed honeydew melon
- 1 cup cubed jicama
- 1 mango, cut into bite-sized pieces
- 1 pear, cut into bite-sized pieces

- 1 tablespoon plus 2 teaspoons vegetable oil
- 1 teaspoon bottled chili sauce
- 1 teaspoon ketchup
- 1 teaspoon oyster sauce
- 1 teaspoon soy sauce
- 1 teaspoon sugar
- 1½ teaspoons apricot jam
- 1½ teaspoons cornstarch
- 2 tablespoons toasted sesame seeds
- 2 teaspoons fine sugar
- 3 tablespoons ground peanuts
- 3 tablespoons water

Directions:

1. In a moderate-sized-sized mixing container, mix the soy sauce, fine sugar, oyster sauce, and 1 tablespoon of the vegetable oil. Put in the shredded duck to the container and toss to coat; set aside.
2. In a small container, whisk together the 3 tablespoons of water, salt, 1 teaspoon of sugar, sesame oil, ketchup, chili sauce, and cornstarch; set aside.
3. In a small deep cooking pan, heat the rest of the vegetable oil on moderate heat. Put in the sauce mixture to the pan and cook until it becomes thick. Mix in the apricot jam and remove the pan from the heat. Cool the sauce in your fridge. Stir before you use.
4. Mound the duck in the middle of a big serving platter. Position the fruits and vegetables around the duck. Ladle the sauce over the duck, fruits, and vegetables. Drizzle the salad with chopped peanuts and sesame seeds. Serve immediately.

Yield: Servings 4–6

SHRIMP "PÂTÉ"

Ingredients:

- ¼ teaspoon white pepper

- ½ teaspoon salt
- 1 red chili, seeded and thoroughly minced (not necessary)
- 1 teaspoon sugar
- 1¼ cups minced shrimp
- 2 tablespoons vegetable oil
- 8 (4-inch) pieces sugarcane Sweet-and-sour or other favorite dipping sauce

Directions:

1. Preheat your oven to 375 degrees.
2. Put the shrimp, salt, sugar, white pepper, and chili in a food processor; process until the desired smoothness is achieved.
3. Sprinkle in one to 2 tablespoons of the vegetable oil. Process the shrimp mixture until it reaches the consistency necessary to make a meatball, using nearly oil.
4. Split the shrimp mixture into 4 equivalent portions.
5. Use your hands to mold a "shrimp ball" around the center of each of the sugarcane pieces.
6. Put the "skewers" on a baking sheet and roast for roughly twenty minutes. If you prefer them a little extra browned, broil them (after they are done baking) until the desired color is reached.
7. To serve, spoon some of the sweet-and-sour sauce into the middle of 4 plates. Put the sugarcane "skewer" on top of the sauce.

Yield: Servings 4

SINGAPORE NOODLES

Ingredients:

- ¼ cup oyster sauce
- 1 package rice sticks, soaked in hot water until tender and drained
- 1–2 teaspoons red pepper flakes
- 2 cups cooked meat or shrimp in bite-sized pieces
- 2 green onions, trimmed and thinly cut
- 2 tablespoons minced ginger

- 2 tablespoons vegetable oil
- 2 teaspoons soy sauce
- 3 tablespoons curry powder
- 4 cloves garlic, minced

Directions:

1. Heat the vegetable oil in a wok or big frying pan on moderate to high heat. Put in the garlic and the ginger. Stir-fry until tender.
2. Put in the cooked meat or shrimp, green onion, and red pepper flakes to the wok; stir-fry until hot.
3. Mix in the oyster sauce, curry powder, and soy sauce. Put in the rice noodles and toss. Serve instantly.

Yield: Servings 2–3

SINGAPORE SHELLFISH SOUP

Ingredients:

- ¼ cup chopped cilantro
- 1 (14-ounce) can coconut milk
- 1 (1-inch) piece ginger, peeled and chopped
- 1 7-ounce package of rice noodles, soaked in hot water until soft
- 1 cup bean sprouts
- 1 pound big raw shrimp, peeled, shells reserved
- 1 pound mussels, cleaned and debearded
- 1 tablespoon anchovy paste
- 1 tablespoon ground coriander
- 1 tablespoon lime zest
- 1 teaspoon turmeric
- 1–2 tablespoons fish sauce
- 2 cloves garlic, minced
- 2 tablespoons vegetable oil, divided

- 3 serrano chilies, seeded and chopped
- 3 stalks lemongrass, outer layers removed, inner core thinly cut
- 4 small shallots, peeled and cut
- 6 big scallops, cut horizontally into 2–3 pieces, depending on their size
- Lime wedges

Yield: Servings 6–8

Directions:

1. In a moderate-sized-sized deep cooking pan heat 1 tablespoon of the oil on moderate to high heat and fry the shrimp shells until pink.
2. Put in 3 cups of water to the pan and bring to its boiling point; decrease the heat and simmer for half an hour Strain the shells from the broth, then boil the broth until it is reduced to 2 cups.
3. In a big frying pan, bring ½ cup of water to its boiling point. Put in the mussels, cover, and allow to steam until opened, approximately five minutes. Discard any mussels that have not opened. Strain the cooking liquid and save for later. Shell all but about of the mussels; set the mussels aside.
4. Put the lemongrass, chilies, garlic, ginger, shallots, anchovy paste, and 2 tablespoons of water in a food processor. Process to make a thick paste, putting in more water if required.
5. Heat the rest of the vegetable oil in a big soup pot on moderate heat. Put in the lemongrass paste and fry, stirring constantly, until mildly browned, approximately ten minutes. Mix in the turmeric and ground coriander and cook for a minute more.
6. Put in the shrimp broth and mussel cooking liquid to the pot, stirring to dissolve the paste. Bring to its boiling point, reduce heat, and simmer for ten to fifteen minutes.
7. Put in the coconut milk and fish sauce; return to its boiling point. Put in the noodles and lime zest; simmer for a couple of minutes. Put in the shrimp and simmer for a couple of minutes more. Put in the scallop slices. After half a minute or so, put in the shelled mussels and bean sprouts. Lightly stir until blended.
8. To serve, ladle the soup into deep soup bowls. Decorate using the mussels in their shells, drizzle with chopped cilantro and the juice from a lime wedge over the top of each container.

SINGAPORE SHRIMP

Ingredients:

- ¼ cup green onion slices
- ¼ teaspoon Chinese 5-spice powder
- 1 can coconut milk
- 1 clove garlic, minced
- 1 cup cut domestic mushrooms
- 1 teaspoon minced ginger
- 1½ pounds cooked shrimp
- 2 tablespoons vegetable oil
- 2 teaspoons hoisin sauce
- 2 teaspoons oyster sauce
- 2 teaspoons Red Curry Paste (Page 17)
- Salt and pepper to taste

Directions:

1. In a wok or big sauté pan, heat the vegetable oil on moderate to high.
2. Put in the mushrooms, green onions, garlic, and ginger; stir-fry for two to three minutes.
3. Mix together the hoisin sauce, oyster sauce, and curry paste, and 5-spice powder until well blended. Put in the mixture to the wok.
4. Mix in the coconut milk and tweak seasoning to taste with the salt and pepper. Put in the shrimp and bring to a simmer. Cook for one to two minutes until the shrimp are thoroughly heated.

Yield: Servings 4

SPICE-POACHED CHICKEN

Ingredients:

- ¼ cup light soy sauce
- ¼ teaspoon dried tangerine peel (dried orange peel can be substituted)

- ½ teaspoon whole black peppercorns
- ½ teaspoon whole cloves
- 1 (2-inch) cinnamon stick
- 1 cardamom pod
- 1 whole star anise
- 2 tablespoons sugar
- 4–6 boneless, skinless chicken breasts
- 5 cups water

Directions:

1. Put the star anise, peppercorns, cloves, cinnamon stick, cardamom pod, tangerine peel, and water in a stew pot. Bring the mixture to its boiling point using high heat. Let boil until the poaching liquid is reduced to 4 cups.
2. Mix in the soy sauce and the sugar. Return the liquid to its boiling point.
3. Put in the chicken breasts and reduce to a simmer. Poach the breasts until done, approximately twenty minutes.

Yield: Servings 4–6

SWEET CAMBODIAN BROTH WITH PORK AND EGGS

Ingredients:

- ½ teaspoon freshly ground black pepper
- ½ teaspoon salt
- 1 big pork tenderloin, cut into bite-sized cubes
- 1 cup fish sauce
- 1 cup sugar
- 1 cup thinly cut bamboo shoots
- 4 cups water
- 5 tablespoons soy sauce
- 6–8 hard-boiled eggs
- Rice, cooked in accordance with package directions

Directions:

1. Bring the water to its boiling point in a big deep cooking pan. Put in the soy sauce, black pepper, salt, sugar, fish sauce, and hard-boiled eggs; simmer for fifteen minutes.
2. Put in the cubed pork and the bamboo shoots and simmer for another thirty minutes.
3. Lower the heat to low, cover, and allow to simmer for two to three hours. Adjust seasonings to taste.
4. To serve, mound some rice on the bottom of soup bowls. Ladle soup over the rice.

Yield: Servings 4–6

SWEET-AND-SOUR VEGETABLES

Ingredients:

- ¼ cup rice vinegar
- 1 big green pepper, seeded and slice into bite-sized pieces
- 1 cup brown sugar
- 1 cup cut carrots
- 1 cup fresh pineapple chunks
- 1 cup unsweetened pineapple juice
- 1 cup water, divided
- 1 onion, cut
- 1 teaspoon grated ginger
- 2 cloves garlic, crushed
- 2 tablespoons cornstarch
- 2 tablespoons soy sauce
- 4 cups broccoli
- 6 green onions, trimmed and slice into 1-inch lengths

Directions:

1. Put the carrots, onion, green pepper, garlic, and ginger in a big deep cooking pan with ½ cup of the water. Bring the water to its boiling point and allow to cook for five minutes, stirring regularly.

2. Put in the broccoli, green onions, and the rest of the ½ cup of water. Bring the water to its boiling point; reduce the heat, cover, and allow to simmer for five minutes.
3. In the meantime, in a small container, meticulously mix the pineapple juice, rice vinegar, soy sauce, brown sugar, and cornstarch.
4. Put in the pineapple juice mixture and the pineapple chunks to the wok. Raise the heat to moderate and cook, stirring continuously, until the sauce becomes thick.

Yield: Servings 6

TAMARIND DIPPING SAUCE

Ingredients:

- ½ teaspoon ground fennel
- 1 cup hot water
- 1 teaspoon ground cumin
- 1 teaspoon salt
- 2 teaspoons brown sugar
- 2 teaspoons grated ginger
- 3 tablespoons tamarind pulp
- Lemon juice to taste

Directions:

1. Put the tamarind pulp in a small container. Pour boiling water over the pulp and allow to soak until soft, approximately fifteen minutes.
2. Break up the pulp and then strain the tamarind water through a fine-mesh sieve, using the back of a spoon to push the pulp through, but leaving the tough fibers.
3. Mix in the rest of the ingredients and let the tamarind sauce sit for minimum fifteen minutes before you serve.

Yield: Approximately 1¼ cups

TANDOORI CHICKEN

Ingredients:

- ½ cup plain yogurt
- ½ teaspoon saffron threads
- 1 tablespoon grated ginger
- 1½ teaspoons <u>Garam Masala</u>
- 2 small garlic cloves, minced
- 2 tablespoons ghee, melted
- 2 teaspoons paprika
- 2 teaspoons salt
- 4 skinless chicken breasts
- 4 skinless chicken legs
- teaspoon chili powder

Directions:

1. Using a small, sharp knife, make three to 4 (¼-inch-deep) slits in each piece of chicken. Set aside in a container big enough to hold all of the pieces.
2. Put the saffron in a small sauté pan on moderate heat and toast for roughly half a minute. Put the saffron on a small plate and let it cool and crumble.
3. Mix the saffron into the yogurt.
4. Grind together the ginger, garlic, garlic, salt, chili pepper, paprika, and garam masala. Mix the spice mixture into the yogurt.
5. Pour the yogurt over the chicken, ensuring that all of the pieces are coated. Cover and marinate overnight flipping the pieces in the marinade every so frequently.
6. Preheat your oven to 450 degrees.
7. Put in the ghee to a roasting pan big enough to hold al of the chicken pieces. Put in the chicken, breast side down. Ladle some of the ghee over the pieces. Roast for about ten minutes. Turn the pieces over, coat again, and continue roasting for five minutes. Turn them again and roast for another five minutes. Turn 1 last time (breasts must be up); coat and cook until done, approximately 5 more minutes.

Yield: Servings 4

TEA-SMOKED CHICKEN

Ingredients:

- ½ cup brown sugar
- ½ cup cooked rice
- ½ cup green tea leaves
- ½ teaspoon salt
- 1 teaspoon sesame oil
- 2 teaspoons rice wine
- 6–8 boneless, skinless chicken breasts

Directions:

1. Swiftly wash the chicken breasts under cold water and pat dry. Drizzle with the salt and rice wine. Set aside in your fridge for half an hour
2. In the meantime, prepare the wok: Coat the bottom using a sheet of aluminium foil. Put the tea leaves, brown sugar, and rice on the bottom of the wok and toss to blend. Place a wire grill rack on the wok.
3. Heat the wok on moderate to high heat. Place the chicken on the rack and cover with a tight-fitting lid. Remove the heat after smoke starts to emit from the wok, but leave it on the burner for about ten minutes or until the chicken is thoroughly cooked.
4. Brush the chicken with the sesame oil. Serve immediately.

Yield: Servings 6–8

TROPICAL FRUITS WITH CINNAMON AND LIME

Ingredients:

- ½ teaspoon sesame oil
- ½–1 teaspoon cinnamon Pinch of salt
- 3 tablespoons honey
- 6 cups of tropical fruits, such as mango, papaya, bananas, melons, star fruit, kiwi, etc., (anything really) cut into bite-sized pieces

- Zest and juice of 6 limes

Directions:

1. Mix the lime zest and all but about of the lime juice in a small container. Slowly sprinkle in the honey, whisking to make a smooth mixture. Whisk in the sesame oil, cinnamon, and salt. Adjust flavor to your preference with more lime juice if required.
2. Put the fruit in a big serving container. Pour the cinnamon-lime dressing over the fruit, toss to blend, and allow to rest in your fridge for fifteen minutes before you serve.

Yield: Servings 6–12

VIETNAMESE BANANAS

Ingredients:

- 1 tablespoon grated ginger Grated zest of 1 orange
- 3 tablespoons brown sugar
- 3 tablespoons butter
- 3 tablespoons shredded coconut (unsweetened)
- 3 teaspoons toasted sesame seeds
- 4 tablespoons lime juice
- 6 bananas, peeled and cut in half along the length
- 6 tablespoons orange liqueur

Directions:

1. Heat a small nonstick pan using high heat. Put in the coconut and cook, stirring continuously, until a golden-brown colour is achieved. Take away the coconut from the pan and save for later.
2. In a big sauté pan, melt the butter on moderate to high heat. Mix in the brown sugar, the ginger, and orange zest. Put the bananas in the pan, cut-side down, and cook for one to two minutes or until the sauce begins to become sticky. Turn the bananas over to coat in the sauce. Put the bananas on a heated serving platter and cover using aluminium foil.

3. Return the pan to the heat and meticulously mix in the lime juice and the orange liqueur. Using a long-handled match, ignite the sauce. Allow the flames to die down and then pour the sauce over the bananas.
4. Drizzle the bananas with the toasted coconut and the sesame seeds. Serve instantly.

Yield: Servings 6

VIETNAMESE OXTAIL SOUP

Ingredients:

- ¼ cup chopped cilantro
- ½ pound bean sprouts
- 1 (7-ounce) package rice sticks, soaked in hot water until tender and drained
- 1 green onion, trimmed and thinly cut
- 1 small cinnamon stick
- 1 tablespoon vegetable oil
- 1 tablespoon whole black peppercorns
- 1 whole star anise
- 2 garlic cloves, peeled and crushed
- 2 limes, cut into wedges
- 2 medium carrots, peeled and julienned
- 2 medium onions
- 3 tablespoons fish sauce
- 4 (½-inch) pieces ginger, peeled
- 4 serrano chilies, seeded and thinly cut
- 5 pounds meaty oxtails
- Freshly ground black pepper to taste

Directions:

1. Cut 1 of the onions into ¼-inch slices. Heat the vegetable oil in a moderate-sized sauté pan on moderate to high heat. Put in the onion slices and sauté until they barely start to brown. Drain the oil from the browned onion and save for later.

2. Slice the rest of the onion into paper-thin slices. Cover using plastic wrap and save for later.

3. Wash the oxtails in cold water and put them in a stock pot. Cover the tails with cold water and bring to its boiling point. Lower the heat and skim any residue that has come to the surface. Let simmer for fifteen minutes.

4. Put in the browned onions, ginger, carrots, cinnamon, star anise, peppercorns, and garlic. Return the stock to a simmer and cook for 6 to 8 hours, putting in water if required.

5. When the broth is done, skim off any additional residue. Take away the oxtails from the pot and allow to cool until easy to handle. Take away the meat from the bones. Position the meat on a platter and decorate it with the cut green onions. Discard the bones.

6. Strain the broth and return to the stove. Put in the fish sauce and black pepper to taste. Keep warm.

7. On a second platter, position the bean sprouts, chopped cilantro, cut chilies, and lime wedges.

8. Bring a pot of water to its boiling point. Plunge the softened rice noodles in the water to heat. Drain.

9. To serve, place a portion of the noodles in each container. Set a tureen of the broth on the table together with the platter of oxtail meat and the platter of accompaniments. Let your guests serve themselves.

Yield: Servings 6–8

VIETNAMESE PORK STICKS

Ingredients:

For the pork:

- ¼ teaspoon Chinese hot chili oil
- ¼ teaspoon sugar
- ½ cup chopped basil
- ½ cup chopped cilantro
- ½ cup chopped mint
- 1 (½-inch) piece ginger, peeled and minced

- 1 clove garlic, minced
- 1 green onion, trimmed and minced
- 1 pound lean ground pork
- 1 tablespoon soy sauce
- 1¼ teaspoons lemon juice
- 12 bamboo skewers, soaked in water
- 12 Boston or leaf lettuce leaves
- 2 teaspoons vegetable oil
- 6 big water chestnuts, minced
- teaspoon salt

For the dipping sauce:

- ½ cup soy sauce
- 1 (1-inch) piece ginger, minced
- 1 teaspoon oyster sauce
- 2 garlic cloves, minced
- 2 teaspoons sugar
- 3 tablespoons water
- 5 tablespoons lemon juice
- Pinch of cayenne pepper

Directions:

1. To prepare the pork: In a big container, use your hands to meticulously mix the ground pork, water chestnuts, garlic, green onion, soy sauce, vegetable oil, lemon juice, ginger, sugar, chili oil, and salt.
2. Split the mixture into 12 portions. Shape each portion into a cylinder about 3 inches by 1 inch. Cautiously insert a bamboo skewer through each cylinder along the length. Set aside.
3. Put the lettuce leaves, cilantro, mint, and basil in 4 separate serving bowls. Place in your fridge until ready to serve.

4. To prepare the dipping sauce: In a small deep cooking pan mix all the sauce ingredients. Bring the mixture to its boiling point on moderate to high heat. Decrease the heat and simmer for five minutes. Take away the sauce from the heat and allow to cool.

5. Prepare a charcoal or gas grill. Put the skewers in a grill basket, ensuring they are tightly held but not squashed. Grill the skewers until the pork is thoroughly cooked and the outside is crunchy, approximately ten to fifteen minutes flipping the basket regularly.

6. To serve, pour each guest some of the dipping sauce into a small individual container. Put the bowls of cilantro, mint, and basil in the center of the table. Put 2 lettuce leaves and 2 pork skewers on each guest's plate.

7. To assemble, have each guest slide the pork from the skewer onto a lettuce leaf. Drizzle the pork with some of the herbs to taste. Roll the lettuce around the pork and dip in the sauce.

Yield: Servings 6

ABOUT THE AUTHOR

Born and brought up in Thailand, Urassaya Manaying is a professional cook and nutritionist who specializes in traditional Thai recipes. She is best known for her cookbooks on Thai Cooking.

Made in the USA
Las Vegas, NV
04 December 2023

82088477R00142